Quit Playing with Fire

Quit Playing with Fire

by
Ron Luce

New Leaf Press

First printing: March 1995
Second printing: August 1995
Third printing: May 1997

Library of Congress Catalog Number: 94-69835
ISBN: 0-89221-280-2

All Scripture in this book is from the New International Version of the Bible.

Dedication

To my son Cameron Townsend Luce.
May my life demonstrate to you the teachings herein.

Acknowledgments

This book has come out of who I really am, and my wife has been the human being who has contributed most to everything that I am. She has added the ingredients to my life that make my life an incredible existence and joy to live. I thank God for you, Katie!

I also want to thank Cindy Powell, my secretary, who has worked countless hours tracking down all the details for this book, and the only robo-intern to ever endure me for a whole year!

Joni Jones has again added her finesse to this manuscript and made me look better than I really do, thank you.

Contents

Introduction

Fire. One of the most essential ingredients for the survival of mankind. Yet, if you get too close to it, or don't take its potency seriously, you will get burned.

Too many teens today are not taking seriously the consequences of playing with fire. They are fooling around with the things of the world that can burn them. They get lured by the illusion that it will be fun, not realizing that the real story is much less glamorous. They try to stay as close to the world as they can without totally falling away. They tango with temptation and end up feeling the sting of sin.

Others play with the fire of God. They halfheartedly go to church and youth group, but never take God seriously unless they are in a crisis. Many really do want the fire of the presence of the living God in their life, but they just don't know how to get it and keep it. They settle for an emotional time at the altar at a retreat, and hope "the feeling" doesn't go away. When it does, they try to get it back, but get tired of going back and forth trying to stay on fire. As a result they get burned out on the "God thing."

It is time to get honest about the issues that are burning teens. It is time to deal with these vital obstacles to living a Christian life from an in-your-face biblical perspective.

It is time to *quit playing with fire,* and get as far away as we can from the world. Teens need real solutions for the real tough times they face. God has these answers in the

Word and they are presented in this book in a way that a teen can understand. This is not a book to make you feel good about what you are doing. It is about getting out of the situations that cause Christian teens to fall on their faces. It is help for specific issues that teens everywhere are wrestling with.

It is time to *quit playing with the fire of God* and get serious about living close to Him every day. You do not have to go back and forth all your teen years in your walk with God. It is time to get hooked into God with all you've got while you are young, and never let go. It is time to get plugged into the power from the Most High God, and never get turned off again.

As we draw closer to the end times, the complexity of the issues that teenagers face is increasing. We know that all the answers come from Scripture, but how do we apply them to the specific situations faced by the teens of the nineties?

Too many teens, who have been in church all of their life, feel like God cannot relate to the problems they are facing on a daily basis. "If this Christian life is so great, then why can't I get it together? Why are so many things falling apart in my life? Where is God when all these things are happening to me?" These are the kinds of questions that young people are asking and need to get some real answers to.

This book addresses many of the key issues that are huge question marks in the minds of teens today. Once all the hype of a Christian event is gone, how do we keep a fire burning for God? It is incredibly important that we stay real with God and let Him help us with the real life issues we face.

It *is* possible to keep your fire burning for God all through your teen years. I know, because I did it. You just have to be willing to have some "in-your-face" answers from God. These are the kinds of answers you will get in *Quit Playing with Fire.*

This book was written so that teens could read it and

apply the principles to their life. It was written so parents would know how to counsel and guide their teens in these issues. The ultimate is to have both parent and teen read through it together and discuss and pray about what they read.

Section I

Breaking the Spiritual Gridlock

The fire of God. What is it? How do you get it? How do you keep it? So many young people "play" when it comes to their relationship with God. They do not get serious until they face a crisis. They are sometimes committed and sometimes not. The fire of God is His undeniable presence in your life! People can see Him in you without you telling them. It is time to quit playing with the fire of God and get serious about getting all of Him that we can living big in us.

The most essential part of dealing with all the tough situations facing your life as a teen is to make sure that the fire of God is continuing to burn strong in your life. It is so easy to go to a camp or conference and *feel God* there, and then return home and feel like nothing happened.

It is time to get serious about your walk with God. If you want Him to help you with all the other intense things you are facing, you have to be pursuing Him with all your heart! You cannot be an air-head Christian and expect God to bless your life. You have to blast through the tendency to be on a spiritual roller coaster.

You might be young, but you are not too young to be serious in your pursuit of God. David, Josiah, Mark, and

Timothy are all biblical examples of young people who were serious about God. You cannot just pray a crisis prayer every time you get into trouble and hope God gets you out of the mess. If you go after Him with all you've got all the time, He will keep you from getting into so many messes!

This first section is written to help you blast through the emotional ups and downs and the distractions, and to stay real with God. If you will apply what you learn to your life, you will never have to live on that spiritual roller coaster again.

1

What Are You Hungry For?

It seems like everyone is looking for something to "fill me up." People are looking for more fun, more adventure, more thrills, more happiness, or more of something else that they just cannot seem to get their hands on.

We, as human beings, are hungry for something to fill the holes in our lives. We have a craving to eat more, have more, and do more. What do you crave more than anything? What do you really want?

The Bible says in Matthew 5:6, "Blessed are those who hunger and thirst for righteousness, for they will be filled."

We are all empty without God's love inside us. It does not matter how cool someone looks on the outside, if he does not know God, then he is empty. It does not matter how much money he has, how popular he is, or how successful he looks. Without Jesus in the middle of your life, you are empty. People try to fill their lives with all kinds of things but only come up empty every time.

Jesus said we should be hungry for righteousness. This means we should be longing for every part of our life to be right with God. We should want God to smile on every part of what we do every day. This includes our hearts, habits, attitudes, friends, free time, feelings, music, movies, school, family, and boyfriend or girlfriend.

Many young people who have been in church for a long time say, "I've been in church for years. I've prayed the prayer and everything. Why am I not filled up?"

Jesus promised that you would be filled, not if you went to church, not if you went to youth group, not if you cried at the last night of camp every year, but only if you were HUNGRY for Him and for righteousness.

To hunger is to crave. It means to strongly desire something. It's about longing for and earnestly, intensely desiring something. It is an eagerness, an inclination, a passion. It is like you are famished and thirsty so that you devour greedily.

Are You Hungry?

What are you craving? The world craves things like what to eat, drink, wear, drive, watch, listen to, and go to. The world craves fun, video games, sports, competition, movies, and the American dream. What teens in America feed themselves is what they are putting in their minds and lives. The average teen:

12 - 17 years of age watches 23 hours of TV per week.[1] By the time a child finishes high school he will have spent 18,000 hours with the TV curriculum and only 12,000 with the school curriculum.[2]

. . . has listened to 10,500 hours of music by the time he is out of twelfth grade;[3]

. . . has seen 18,000 murders on television by the time they reach high school graduation.[4]

. . . sees an estimated 14,000 sexual references and innuendoes per year on television.[5]

. . . has seen 100,000 beer commercials by age 18.[6]

These are just some of the things that are filling the minds and hearts of teens all over America and around the world. Most young people end up feeding themselves a lot of "junk food" for their head and heart. Junk food gives you the illusion of being full, but you are still empty. These things will destroy, or at the very least distract you from your relationship with God.

The world fills itself up so much with all this stuff that they forget to hunger for God. The problem is that sometimes we, who call ourselves Christians, also fill ourselves with these very same things. Those of us who say we love God forget to hunger for more of Him! As a result we get so satisfied with mediocrity that we think we are doing pretty good as a Christian. We forget to passionately pursue our Saviour.

Many teens who go to youth group every week see so many movies, videos, and other music magazine "cool" stuff that they start thinking a star is practically a saint if he mentions God in a song, or the idea of heaven or angels in a movie or video. We know that we have been brainwashed and are mediocre when we start getting our ideas of heaven from Hollywood and from rock music.

We end up thinking that the whole Bible, even though it is the truth, just seems like a fairy tale. The world mocks it so much that you just start believing what they say and start filling your brain with their way of thinking all the time.

It's Time to Blow Some Chunks

If you have been eating all this junk, you need to throw up. You need to get it out of your life. It is time to get rid of the garbage that has been filling our lives and get hungry for God again. We get so full of the junk that there is no room to really hunger for Him.

How do you get the garbage out? You throw it up and get it out by repenting and asking Him to forgive you. It is time to start doing what Jesus said in Matthew 6:33, "Seek first his kingdom and his righteousness, and all these things will be given to you as well."

Are You Really Hungry?

Are you as hungry for God as David was? He wrote in

Psalm 42:1, ". . . As the deer pants for streams of water, so my soul pants for you. . . ." Do you really long for God? Is your heart dry and thirsty? It is time to take a drink of the right stuff. A drink of God.

David wrote, ". . . Oh God, you are my God, earnestly I seek you; my soul thirsts for you, my body longs for you, in a dry and weary land where there is no water" (Ps. 63:1). Do you earnestly want more of God in your life? A lot of people just go to church and then go home. They want to just barely make it to heaven. No wonder they are empty on the inside. When was the last time you honestly sought God with all of your guts?

David wrote, "My soul yearns, even faints, for the courts of the Lord; my heart and my flesh cry out for the living God" (Ps. 84:2). He was passionately desiring to be as close as he possibly could to God. Do you want Him like that?

Psalm 34:8 says, "Taste and see that the Lord is good. . . ." Are you satisfied with only one taste? After going to a restaurant one time, you may decide that when you return you want to try something different from their menu. Each time you return you try a different meal.

This is exactly what many teens do in their walk with God. They "try" Him at a camp. Then they go back to the world and taste a little of everything else on the menu. They try a little drinking, drugs, and immorality. They think they got all of God because they "tasted" what it was like one time. It is time for us to *fill up* on Him. If you just try Him or taste a little, you will still be hungry for more. You will have to have more of Him or you will try to fill up on other things.

Things to Hunger For

To hunger for God is to hunger for the Word of God, the truth. We need to hunger for His guidance, hunger to have more love for Him burning in our hearts. We should be longing to understand His Word, to have His fire blazing out of control in our lives. We ought to want Him to use us; we need to long for awesome prayer times. We should yearn to know His purpose in our life, the depth of His love, and how He thinks. We should have a craving to treat people like Jesus did. We should hate sin and have an intense desire to see miracles every day. We should have an uncontrollable urge to REALLY KNOW HIM.

It is time to feed ourselves in a big way. It is time to stuff ourselves on God. Right now, fill up on Him. Do something about it! When I was still a teen I went so crazy about seeking Him that I read the entire Bible in six weeks. I challenge you to do the same!

Are You Desperate?

The TV and newspapers have shown time and time again that famine has broken out in countries around the world. The fathers are trying to work to get food for their wives and children, but none is available. Finally they begin to rob and steal from others. They are not common criminals, they are just hungry. I have even heard of a gang of men stealing powdered milk from an orphanage to get food for their own children. THESE MEN WERE DESPERATE.

Are You Desperate for God Like That?

Are you willing to do whatever it takes to find Him?

I saw many starving children in India. Many of them beg in the street all day long just trying to get food to live. However, in the same country, there are those who will take a whole platter of nicely diced vegetables and offer them to an idol. They will place the vegetables before the idol and let them lie there and rot as a sacrifice to that god. They could eat the food and be healthy themselves, or feed it to their own starving children, but instead they just let it rot.

It seems like a lot of starving Christians do the same thing. They have plenty of opportunities to eat the Word of God. The pastor is preaching with all his heart and teens sit there writing notes to their friends. God could have fed them, even longed to feed them, but they refused to eat. We could read the Bible like crazy, listen to tapes, and ask our leaders questions if we really wanted to learn more. Instead, we often starve to death spiritually. We get pulled into ritualistic Christianity. We are all caught up in doing good things to put on a show that we are spiritual, but we forget to hunger for God. We want God's blessing, especially when we are in trouble, but do we want Him?

It Is Time for a Feast

The Bible says, ". . . man does not live on bread alone but on every word that comes from the mouth of the Lord" (Deut. 8:3). You cannot really be alive until you get God's Word in you. Physical bread cannot satisfy a hungry heart. Jesus said, ". . . I am the bread of life . . ." (John 6:35).

If you want real life, you have to have real bread.

God promises to fill you if you will just hunger for righteousness. If you are tired of feeling like an empty person or an empty Christian, just get hungry for Him. He will fill you with himself, and you can take that to the bank!

WHAT TO DO: PRAY A PRAYER OF REPENTANCE TO GET ALL THE GARBAGE OUT OF YOUR LIFE THAT HAS BEEN FILLING YOUR MIND AND YOUR HEART. THEN YOU SHOULD DO SOMETHING TO BEGIN TO FILL YOURSELF WITH HIM AND HIS WORD. MAKE A COMMITMENT TO FORCE–FEED YOURSELF THE WORD OF GOD NOW.

2

Are You Alive? Taking Your Spiritual Pulse

Most young people who have been around church for any length of time know what it means to be hyped up for God. They have been to camps and retreats that get their emotions all stirred up, and they leave hoping to stay stirred up. When they discover that their excitement has waned, looking for the next chance to get the "spiritual goose bumps" becomes the focus of their spiritual life. Going from highs to lows is not what a normal Christian life is supposed to be about. It is not about whether you are stirred up or not. The Bible says that Jesus came that we ". . . may have life, and have it to the full" (John 10:10). He did not come to stir us up emotionally, but to give us life.

How can you tell if you have that real life inside you? There are a lot of people who are walking around with living bodies on the outside, but they are dead on the inside. They are walking dead people, the "living dead." They are dry on the inside — lonely, empty, weary, and spiritually tired.

Of course, we know people who have never given their life to the Lord are just like this. They act like they are living, but on the inside they are dead. The only way for their heart to "come alive" is by giving it to Jesus. The problem is that a lot of people who *have* given their lives to Jesus still seem dry and dead. That is why they keep trying to get the emotional highs at events. An emotional high is just a substitute for the real life God wants to fill us with.

Christians ought to be the most alive people you have ever met in your life. When someone meets you and looks in your eyes he ought to see something that is real inside of you. When he reaches out to shake your hand, he should be grabbing hold of something that is really living.

As Christians, we have been forgiven. Our heart is clean. He has given us a future. Our past is forgotten. We are sons and daughters of the BIG G! We can hear His voice! We are not dead anymore. We realize that to live a pure and holy life gives us real life. We can live this life because His power lives inside us!

The question is, do you have this kind of life inside you? Here are a few ways to check your spiritual barometer to see if you are alive:

1. Are Your Roots Deep?

We know from the parable of the sower (Matt. 13) that our roots must be deep if we want to stay alive. If you want your tree to grow (your spiritual tree), you have to have deep roots in the Lord.

A tree must have at least one deep tap root to keep the water coming to the rest of its branches. If it does not, at times of drought, the tree will die. The same is true for you. Your roots must be deep in God's Word so that when you don't have those "hype times," you still have life in you.

How do you get deep roots? By putting the Word of God in your heart and mind. "Blessed is the man [whose] . . . delight is in the law of the Lord, and on his law he meditates day and night. He is like a tree planted by streams of water . . ." (Ps. 1:1-3).

If you meditate on God's Word, He will give you real life in your heart. You can't completely understand it with your mind. But the truth is, when you get His Word in your mind, and you meditate on it like a cow chews his cud, He gives you an unending burst of LIFE!

It is time to get serious about reading the Bible. Every single day, don't just read some — memorize some of what you read! Take one Scripture and chew on it all day long, every single day. What about reading through the whole Bible? Get serious about getting your roots deep in the Word, and you will constantly have real life.

2. Are You Nourished?

Some people eat all the time but are not healthy. They eat, but because they eat junk food, they are weak and sickly.

Many Christians are like this. They go to church and even read their Bibles. But because they do not take seriously what they read, or what they hear, they are malnourished. They think that because they do the activity, they will be healthy. They wonder why they keep falling so easily into sin and bad habits. They go through the spiritual activities but they don't have any spiritual LIFE bursting in their heart.

One great way to get this spiritual nutrition is to fast. The idea is that you do not eat physically, but you do eat spiritually. In fact, you pig-out on God! A fast is really a feast!

Jesus said in Matthew 6:16, "When you fast . . ." not *if* you fast. In other words He expects us to fast. It is a time of getting away from everything and everyone to get tight with God and let Him give you nutrients to live on.

3. Are You Reproducing?

You don't have to force an apple tree to give apples. It just does because it is a living apple tree. You do not have to trick it or beg it to give you apples. It does it naturally if it is alive. Anything that is alive reproduces.

Have you reproduced the life of God inside you and given it to someone else? Are you bearing good fruit?

Some Christians try to convince you and make you feel obligated to share the gospel with other people. But the fact is that if you really have that LIFE burning inside you, you will not be able to keep it to yourself.

Nobody should have to beg you to tell others about God. In fact, if you have this burning life, it will naturally come out, just as the apple trees naturally give apples. People should be asking you to shut up because you are talking so much about Him!

Jesus said, "I am the vine; you are the branches. If a man remains in me and I in him, he will bear much fruit . . ." (John 15:5). If you are really alive, you will be bearing fruit and reaching others for Jesus.

4. Are Your Branches Dead?

The final thing that we can do to check our spiritual pulse is simply to check our branches. Look at your life and ask yourself, "Do I have any dead stuff on me?"

The Bible says, "For the wages of sin is death . . ." (Rom. 6:23). That means that if there is any dead stuff in our life, then we must have let a little sin in there.

Jesus said, ". . . My Father . . . cuts off every branch in me that bears no fruit, while every branch that does bear fruit he prunes so that it will be even more fruitful" (John 15:1-2).

The way a farmer gets rid of dead branches on his vines is to cut them off. That is exactly how we get rid of sin in our life. We must cut if off. Sin kills you! It snuffs the vitality right out of your Christian life. We wonder why it is so hard to really hear from God. When we let sin in, we let death in. We can go to church every week and read our Bible all the time, but if we let sin in we let death in. That is why so many go to church but still do not feel alive on the inside. Once you cut the dead branches off, you will feel the freedom of real forgiveness and real life!

How do you cut them off? Repent and ask forgiveness. Do not ever do it again. Think of every dead branch in your life right now. Take some time to ask God to forgive you. Ask Him to pour the LIFE of His forgiveness into you now.

Let us "go and sin no more," just like Jesus told the woman caught in her sin. Let us be the ones who show this world what real life is all about. You should be the most ALIVE person that anyone has ever met; begin TODAY!

3

The Radical Lordship of Jesus

So many people say that they want to live for Jesus. They love to say how much they love Him and are excited to scream His name loudly at youth conferences.

The problem is: What happens when it is all over? Are you as serious about God the rest of the week as you were at the conference or at church?

There are a lot of people who want to be excited for Jesus. They keep returning to places like concerts and camps where they know they will get a spiritual high. The problem is, the Bible NEVER TELLS US TO BE EXCITED ABOUT JESUS.

The Bible talks a lot about commitment. When we chase after excitement, it is like chasing after the wind. You can never catch it. You cannot keep your excitement forever, but you *can* keep your commitment forever.

We need to chase after God, and He will keep our hearts fired up!

We hear people talking about Jesus being their Lord, but what does that really mean? We hear "Jesus is Lord" screamed at a rally, but very few really live like He is their Lord. What He wants is not people who scream about His lordship, but people who commit to His lordship. Obey it. Live it. It is time for us to stop making a lot of noise about it and just do it: submit to the radical lordship of Jesus.

WHY?

1. Because of Our Love for God

Matthew 22:37 says that you should, ". . . Love the Lord your God with all your heart and with all your soul and with all your mind." We are talking about loving God with all that you are, with everything you have inside of you. This is serious Christianity.

To love Him is to love His ways (how He does things), even when we do not understand why. It's like you say, "God, I know Your Word is true. Even though I don't understand why, I'm going to do it anyway because I love You and trust You."

Jesus said, "If you love me, you will obey what I command" (John 14:15). This is our opportunity to demonstrate our love for God. We cannot simply do lip service and tell Him we love Him; we must do something to show Him we love Him. Some people talk about it. We need to be the ones who live it.

We throw the word "love" around so much that it is hard to know what it means any more. For example, we say that we love pizza. We eat it like crazy, so we say we love it. Then we say that we love God, and we think it is the same thing. According to Jesus, loving God means obeying His commandments and submitting to His lordship.

2. Because There Are Great Advantages in Jesus' Radical Lordship

Romans 6:23 says, "For the wages of sin is death, but the gift of God is eternal life in Christ Jesus our Lord." When you sin you earn wages. You earn death. As soon as you sin, death begins to creep into your life. Your heart gets cold. You get lonely and depressed. You dry up on the inside. This is true even if you are a Christian. If you live in sin, your life shrivels around you.

However, if you live a godly life you will have real life on the inside! Jesus came to give us life, but we will not have it if we play games in our walk with Him.

Romans 6:16 says, ". . . you are slaves to the one whom you obey. . . ." That means that if you obey sinful desires, you become a slave to those desires. Many Christians are in partial slavery. They say they love God, but they keep on obeying sinful desires. They wonder why it is so hard to hear from God, yet they refuse to get all of their life in submission to Him.

The word "Lord" means: boss, chief, the guy you report to, the dude in charge of your life. Got the idea? If we say we are committed to the Lord but do our own thing, it is a joke we are playing only on ourselves. If you are having troubles in your life, examine yourself to see if you are really submitting to Jesus in every area. He promised to bless your face off and give you real life if you really make Him the boss of every area of your life.

If you take drugs, then you are submitting control of your life to them. If you drink alcohol, then you are a slave to a liquid that influences how you think. If you follow your hormones and get into immorality, you are a slave to those hormones just like an animal.

Jesus gives us great advantages when we submit to Him. He promised to set us free from this slavery to sin. John 8:36 says, "So if the Son sets you free, you will be free indeed." Satan cannot boss you around any more!

When you really submit to Him, He starts making everything work together for your good (Rom. 8:28). Life starts making sense again. He also takes away the pain and sting of sin in our lives as we bring every area of our life to Him.

It costs you everything you have to follow God, BUT THE BENEFITS ARE AWESOME!

3. He Demands that We Submit to His Lordship

Jesus said, "Not everyone who says to me, 'Lord, Lord,' will enter the kingdom of heaven, but only he who does the will of my Father who is in heaven" (Matt. 7:21). If He is really our boss, why don't we obey Him? It would be like having a job at McDonald's and going to Burger King and saying, "Hi, Boss, how are you doing?" He would say, "You don't work here, why are you calling me your boss?" You can say "Boss" all you want; if you don't work there, he is not your boss. You can call Jesus your Lord all day long, but if you don't submit to Him, He is not your Lord.

In fact, you do not have the right to call Him your Lord unless you have submitted everything to Him. Paul said it this way, "You were bought at a price . . ." (1 Cor. 6:20). He figured that Jesus had bought him, so He owned him. That is what happens when we give our life to Jesus — He takes full ownership. We no longer have the right to say what we are going to do or where we are going to go.

It is like joining the army. As long as you are enlisted, they own you. Everything you do must have their approval first. This is what it is like to give your life to the Lord, only it is more intense. He not only cares about what you do, but also about what you are. He does not want to change just your actions, but your heart motives and thoughts as well.

THIS IS THE RADICAL LORDSHIP OF JESUS: submission in every part of your life!

Jesus showed us a great example of how to live a submitted life. The Bible says, ". . . he learned obedience from what he suffered" (Heb. 5:8). It also says, "Because he himself suffered when he was tempted . . ." (Heb. 2:18). Jesus knew what it was like to really want to do something sinful. Then part of Him would say, "No way! You can't do that, You're the Son of God!" But part of Him still felt like sinning.

He suffered when He was tempted the same way that you and I suffer. The battle in our mind to say "no" is where we suffer. The Bible says Jesus learned obedience because EVERY TIME He suffered from that battle in the mind, He said NO! He learned obedience because EVERY TIME He got a chance He turned it down, and He obeyed His Father. Paul describes how Jesus became obedient to death (Phil. 2:8).

The great thing is that God gives us the same power today! The Bible says in Titus 2:11–12, "For the grace of God . . . teaches us to say 'No' to ungodliness and worldly passions. . . ." Every time you get tempted you need to remember that God has given you the power to say NO! NO! NO! You are not a slave to sin any longer! He has set you free!

How to Get Out of Slavery

There are two steps to get out of slavery to sin. The first is to ask forgiveness. Most people know that they should do this, but this is usually where they stop.

The second step is to repent. This is not the same as asking for someone's forgiveness. No, it does not mean that you go and cry at the altar a long time. To repent means to change your mind about something. To slam on the brakes and go the other direction is a good analogy. It means that you put your foot down and decide that you will no longer do the same thing you have been doing. It means that you finally realize that the devil has no right to tell you what to do. God has given you the power to say "no," and that is exactly what you do when you repent. No more Mister Nice Guy to the devil. Repenting should be a time of rejoicing because you realize that you are no longer a slave! You are free and you exercise your freedom by walking away from sin.

This is living under the radical lordship of Jesus. It is repenting and living free from sin with Jesus as the boss of your life. Do you need to repent today? Are there things that you have struggled with for a long time? Have you wondered if you will ever be free? You have the key to all freedom right in front of you. It is time to ask forgiveness. It is time to put your foot down and repent. It is time to live under the radical lordship of Jesus!

Make a list right now of the things in your life that you

need to get rid of, the things of which you need to repent. Take some time right now to deal with them and kick them out of your life. It is time to start living FREE! Put your foot down today and refuse to be a slave to sin!

4

Revolution Time: Keeping the Fire in Your Quiet Times

You may have heard that if you want to keep your fire for God burning brightly, you must keep reading your Bible and praying. To most teens, this sounds like the perfect thing to do if you want to get more sleep.

Of course, we need to read our Bibles and pray. But how can we keep it alive and relate it to our lives?

With all the hustle and bustle it is easy to get away from our commitment to really seek God. That commitment seemed so real at the altar. There you were, crying your eyes out to God. You made a radical commitment to Him. You just knew He was there. You knew that you would never be the same. If that moment could only last forever. . . .

But now it is 6:30 in the morning and you do not feel God's presence at all. You feel like you are extra holy just because of the fact you are up early, since most people you know do not even do that. It does not take long to begin to go through the motions. You read your Bible and pray because you are SUPPOSED to do those things to be a good

Christian, but you don't get much out of your time. WHY? WHY? WHY? It *was* real! What happened?

The question is: If you are getting up to seek God, are you finding Him? You felt close to Him before, but now it is a distant memory. Let me venture to say that God did not leave. If someone moved it was you. We need to break through the spiritual ritual and get real with Him. He does not want us just to do the spiritual-looking thing. He wants us to really BE SPIRITUAL. The point of your quiet time is to connect with God. If you do not connect, your time is wasted.

It only takes about 24 hours for your relationship with God to get stale. You have to do things to keep it alive or it will seem dry. Here are some specific things to keep your quiet times alive, and to keep you connected to God:

1. Examine Your Heart

The first thing to do is to make sure your heart is totally clean before God. Is there anything in there He would not be proud of? Have you done or thought anything since the last time you got tight with God? Is there anything in there that has built a wall between you and God?

Just ask Him to show you any area of your heart that is not pleasing to Him. Ask Him to show you what is blocking your relationship with Him. Ask Him to reveal to you any sin you may have in your heart that He is wanting you to repent of.

It is amazing how God will begin to speak to you when you ask these kinds of questions. He is wanting so much to be connected to you, all you have to do is ask the right questions. Too many people sit in their quiet times day in and day out never really hearing God's voice. He will open the windows of heaven and speak to you like a bolt of lightning if you sincerely want to hear. Once you have heard what He wants you to change, go for it. Stand up like a man or woman of God and repent. Get rid of it!

Once the sin is taken care of, you will begin to hear His voice in all kinds of other areas. You will hear His voice about your future. The Scripture will come alive to you. You will have a clear line to the heart of God.

2. Choose to Worship Him No Matter How You Feel

You have to make a determination to worship your face off even if you do not feel like it. You have to realize that no matter how you feel, He is still GOD! Whether you had a good day or not, He is still the Creator of the universe. He is worthy of all our heart singing to Him with everything in us no matter how we feel.

The Bible says, "Enter his gates with thanksgiving and his courts with praise . . ." (Ps. 100:4). If you want to get into God's presence there is only one way to get there. You cannot beg to get in. You cannot just hope to get in. You must worship your way in.

You must be determined to go for it. Do not be satisfied with having just a "pretty good time" with God. You have to go all the way. Sing to Him with all you have, even if you are the only one around. Grab some of the psalms and read them to God as if you wrote them yourself. Read them, or shout them, as if they are coming from your heart! Say it until you mean it. You will be amazed at what will happen in your quiet times when you are determined to enter into real worship: God will show up and blow your face off.

3. Be Creative When You Are Reading Your Bible

What do I mean by this? Do not just sit down and read and then shut the book. Many people cannot remember what they read, even right after they read it. Here are some ideas to make it creative and to help you get some real meat out of God's word.

A. Read through an entire book at once. Do not just skip around from book to book of the Bible. Ask yourself, who was He writing to? What did He really mean when He wrote it? What did they think it meant (the people He was writing to)? Many study Bibles have an introduction to each book of the Bible. Be sure to read this; it will help you know a little more about why the person wrote the book. Then ask yourself, "What is God speaking to me today through this?"

B. Study the Bible by theme. Get your concordance and look up a word finding where it is used in all different places in the Bible. For example look up the word FORGIVE, and read all the different passages about forgiveness. God can completely change your life as you really learn about different issues by topic.

C. Read the same thing in the Word that a close friend is reading. For example make a commitment to read through the New Testament together. As you are both reading through Matthew together, write down questions you have about each chapter. When you get together ask each other the questions you have and help each other understand what God is saying. Or both of you could bring your questions to one of your parents or youth leaders. Ask each other, "What did God teach you this morning?" See how God is speaking to both of you in different ways.

D. Find a devotional book to read through. Do not let this be a substitute for the Bible, but get one that will guide you through the Bible. Find one that will help you understand more of the Word and apply it to your life. You could even get the same devotional book with a friend and work through it together. Just as before, ask each other what God is speaking to each of you every morning. There are many different devotional books like this available. You may want to use one that I wrote called *56 DAYS ABLAZE.*

E. When you read through the Scripture, be looking for more of God. Look to see if you can understand more about His personality in each chapter. Ask questions like, "Why did God say that?" or "Why did God do that?" Look for His character traits in every book of the Bible. Every single chapter will teach you more about how He does things. It is like you are on a quest for more of God. Sit down to read with a determination to discover more of who He is. Sit down with a hearty appetite to eat manna from heaven. Just pray and ask Him to open your eyes and show you more of himself. Then watch out!

F. Find one Scripture from what you read each morning and write it down. Memorize it during the day. Take it with you everywhere you go. Chew on it all day long, just like chewing gum. Ask God what you can apply to your life from that Scripture. What does He want you to change TODAY?

4. Ask God for His Compassion for the People of the World

Do you really care for the people around you? Are you reaching out to them? What about the lost around the world? Do you care that they are lost? It is time to be really honest with these questions. We know that we *should* care, but sometimes we still do not care.

You need to share your feelings about the lost with the Lord. Be really honest with Him. Ask Him to fill your heart with compassion like Jesus had. The Bible says, "When he saw the crowds, he had compassion on them . . ." (Matt. 9:36). Ask Him to fill your heart with the same compassion. The Bible also says that ". . . God has poured out his love into our hearts . . ." (Rom. 5:5). Ask Him to let that love, since it is already in you, be known in your head. Ask Him to let you see people through His eyes. Read about people from other countries and pray for them seriously. You might want to get a book called *Operation World* by Patrick Johnstone[7] to help you pray specifically.

5. Make a Commitment to Do It!

Now it is time to set an appointment time with God and keep it. Don't you dare let anything keep you from your time with God! This is more important than school, friends, or fun. It is more important than a movie or meeting with the president of the United States. It is with GOD!

Set a time to get up each morning. Then set your alarm and peel yourself out of bed! Splash cold water on your face. Tell yourself, "WAKE UP!! You have an appointment with the BIG G!"

I remember when I first did this. The first morning came so early. I thought the alarm clock sounded like a demon. I was delirious. But I forced myself to get up and seek God. I made a commitment that no matter how late I stayed up the night before, I would still get up and meet with GOD. If I got tired later in the day, that would be too bad. I would just have to learn to go to bed earlier. I have missed very few times in over 14 years since I made that commitment.

When God sees that you are really serious about seeking Him, He will open up the windows of heaven. He wants to know you aren't just doing another Christian ritual. Keep it alive, keep it real, stay honest with Him each day. Get serious about going after Him with all your heart every time you open the Bible.

The most important thing is that you are real with God each morning. Do not fall into a rut of looking spiritual because you read your Bible. It is time to get serious about seeking God. It is time to quit playing Christian games. We don't want to look spiritual, we want to *be* spiritual, because we discovered more of God this morning!

I commit to get up every morning like Jesus did (Mark 1:35) to meet with God and seek Him with all my heart. I will read my Bible and pray during these times to grow more like Jesus each day.

_____

signed

_____

date

Section II

The Boy/Girl Thing: Date 'em or Hate 'em?

The fire of passion is something that is so alluring for young people. It seems so mysterious and exciting that many teens play with it and get burned. Their hearts get burned, their emotions crushed, and many times their future ruined. They just had to try to touch the fire and were sorry later.

One of the biggest pitfalls to a teenager and his walk with God is the whole dating scene. It seems that if you have a dating relationship, that is all you think about. And if you don't have one, that is all you think about (the one you wish you had). It seems no one knows how to have great Christian friends of the opposite sex.

It is time to get serious about our walk with God and what He says about the boyfriend/girlfriend thing. I have talked to so many young people who were doing great with God until they got into a dating relationship and became distracted.

Like a young man I knew, let's call him John. He got radically committed to the Lord when he was 16. He was plugged into the youth group real strong, but then began to date girls who were not saved, trying to reach them. He got tricked by the American dating system, thinking he "needed" a girlfriend. He ended up weeping bitterly after having compromised his virtue by having sex with a girl. The same mistakes are made even when teens date others in the youth group. Fortunately, John came back to the Lord, and got his life right. Not everyone makes it back, and that is the real tragedy.

This is not just a few *nice ideas* for you to think about. These next few chapters could determine your spiritual survival.

What you have here is not the answers to: "How far is it okay to go on a date?" These are not candy coated answers. We have to quit trying to stay as close as we can to the gates of hell without falling in!

We cannot take a Christian version of what the world is doing and think that it is God's best. God has radically different ideas, and His ideas of dating will save your heart from getting crushed, keep your body pure until marriage, and keep you fired up spiritually.

5

Sex: Seven Reasons to Wait

The '90s are plagued with the notion that everybody is fooling around before marriage. The way that movies and TV programs depict sex outside of marriage, you feel like you are not normal if you wait. Hollywood glamorizes immorality, making it seem like anyone who wants to have any kind of *real life* has to fool around before he gets married. They only show the "exciting" or passionate side of sex without showing the truth of what happens inside someone's heart when he gets involved sexually before marriage.

God is looking for fired–up young people who love Him with all they've got and who will stand up for Him and live pure lives dedicated to Him. No longer should you ashamedly have to look down as if you are embarrassed for being a virgin. There are a lot of great reasons to stay pure. The teens who aren't virgins should be the ones who are ashamed, not you. They are the ones who have blown it, not you! Following are seven of the most obvious reasons.

1. You Could Be Dating Your Pastor's Wife

As young people begin to date, no one seems to take it

seriously. They do not think about who the person they are dating might marry someday. I know a pastor who has his wife's high school boyfriend in his congregation. Sometimes he says from the pulpit, "Someone here used to date my wife!" That might sound kind of wild, but it is true. The person you date will be *someone's* wife or husband someday. Treat him or her like you want your future spouse to be treated.

The Bible says in 1 Timothy 5:2 that we should treat the younger women in the church (your youth group) as sisters with absolute purity. How would you treat your sister? It is pretty sick to think about anything but a pure relationship with your own sister.

You and your sister in your youth group have the same Father. He sees everything you do. How would you feel if you had a daughter and you found out that someone was fooling around with her? What would you want to do to him? Imagine how your Heavenly Father would feel if you were fooling around with your own sister. How do you think He feels when someone is fooling around with *His* daughter?

2. Date 'em and Hate 'em

Most teens do not know how to have a real friendship with someone of the opposite sex. When we have a close friend we usually say, "I know him too well to date him." Studies show that one of the primary reasons that teens date is to fulfill their desire for companionship. They are looking for good friends who care about them. They are fooled into thinking that "the farther I go with this person, the better friends we will be."

Just the opposite is true. After a few dates, kissing substitutes for real communication. Before long, more sexual involvement follows with the hope that it will make you closer. So, here is the all–too–common scenario on most weekends: you go on a date feeling lonely or that you really want to talk, but then you start fooling around; instead of finding the companionship you were seeking, you end up emptier than you began. The very thing you want out of the relationship (a real friendship) is the very thing that physical involvement makes impossible! As you make a commitment and stay away from any immorality before marriage, you will have a much greater possibility of having a *real friendship* with the person you date. The closeness you really want is impossible to find if you get involved sexually. Sex will enhance the closeness a couple has only *after* they are married. It enhances it because they already had a close friendship BEFORE they were married and they chose to wait and do it God's way. If you do not have a heart–to–heart friendship with a person, having sex with him will not give it to you. Getting physical at all before marriage will only destroy your relationship. This seems illogical to the world, but it is the truth.

3. Looking for Love in All the Wrong Places

Many young people think that if they could finally experience sexual intimacy, then they would find real love. Countless young ladies have heard the words, "If you love me, you'll let me. . . ." In a desperate hope for someone who really cares, many have compromised their virtue.

As a result, emptiness and depression begin to hound the love–starved teen. The love and acceptance that you desire cannot be found in a passionate moment of immorality. True love respects a person's purity. Someone may ask, "If it's really love, is it okay?" If it was real love, he would not even ask you.

If sex equaled love, then prostitutes would be the happiest people in the world! As it turns out, they are some of the most miserable people in the world. Many times, teenage girls, looking for the love and acceptance that they wish their father would give them, make desperate attempts to get it from another guy. They come up feeling emptier and worse every time.

4. Can't Look 'em in the Eye

The big question young ladies ask themselves when they are about to lose their purity is, "Will he respect me in the morning?" The answer is always NO! And worse still, you won't respect yourself either.

Sex in the context of marriage is pure and holy and there is nothing to be ashamed of. Genesis 2:25 says, "The man and his wife were both naked, and they felt no shame." Once they had sinned, the Bible says, they realized they were naked and sewed fig leaves together for clothes (Gen. 3:7).

After giving away the precious gift of your purity in an immoral situation there is only one way you can feel: ashamed. Many people feel ugly or dirty or like a dark cloud follows them around wherever they go. It is nothing to be proud of, even for guys. So what if you have hormones, so do dogs! A real man will control himself and treat a young lady with respect.

Many teens begin to see their entire walk with God erode because they are so ashamed of their sexual activities. It is amazing to think that a quick minute of passion could make someone turn his back on God and miss heaven. I hope you do not take the chance.

When I was a youth pastor, there was a girl in my youth group; she was about 18 years old. Jennifer (not her real name) acted like the cutest thing that God ever made. She tried to look spiritual, but also had a seductive side to her. She sort of tried to look cute to constantly attract guys, but acted like it was totally innocent.

It turns out that Jennifer got pregnant by a guy she had been dating (an older guy, because that is . . . cool?) who did not even go to church — much less love the Lord. After she found out that she was going to have a baby, everything changed. She got up in front of the church and apologized. She was sorry she *got caught,* not that she did it in the first place. She dropped out of youth group, and eventually out of church. After she had the baby she continued in her old ways of trying to get the attention of guys. She has struggled with her walk with God ever since.

5. It's a Matter of Life and Death

We all know about sexually transmitted diseases (STDs),

but we think it could never happen to us. There are 25 STDs that are a lot more rampant than we like to think.[8] The facts are that 7,000 people die each year from STDs![9] Gonorrhea is contracted by 1.8 million people each year.[10] There has been a 67 percent increase in syphilis in teens since 1985.[11] Syphilis, passed through sex or birth, can be deadly if left untreated.[12] Five hundred thousand new cases of herpes, which is excruciatingly painful, are reported each year. Once infected with a herpes simplex virus, you're infected for life.[13] WHO estimates 10-12 million people have been infected with the HIV virus over the past decade, and the figure may reach 40 million by the year 2000.[14] This all sounds pretty scary, and maybe even hopeless, but it will never happen to you if you follow God's plan and wait till marriage.

The world tries to tell you that as long as you practice "safe sex," everything will be okay. Their idea is, of course, to use condoms. The fact is that at least one out of every ten condoms is defective. This means that at least once out of every ten times you have sex, you are putting your life at risk. I think you are smarter than that.

6. Worth the Wait

God designed sex to be experienced only in the context of marriage. He knew it would take the love that only a lifelong commitment can bring to get the most satisfaction.

Sex was God's idea! He invented it. He knows how it will be the best! Imagine God and Jesus thinking of how to make humans reproduce. I cannot help thinking one looked at the other and said, "NO WAY, ARE YOU SERIOUS?" The other said, "WAY!" God wants you to have an awesome sex life, and the best way is to be with only one person your whole life. That's it. No regrets, no shame, only pure sexual intimacy the way it was designed to be experienced: in marriage!

The world has already blown it, so, of course, they are going to tell you to go for it before marriage. How would they know how great it could be getting married as a virgin?

In fact, why do we listen to what they say about sex anyway? They are experts on sex, and they don't even know the God who created it? How could they know anything about it that we would want to know or try?

7. *God Said So*

We have established a lot of common sense reasons not to fool around before marriage. But just in case common sense does not make sense to you, here is the best reason: God says so.

First Corinthians 6:19 says that your body is the temple of the Holy Spirit. You have God living in you (assuming that you have given your life to Jesus). You cannot take God's vessel (YOU) and get it involved in sin. First Corinthians 6:18 says to flee from sexual immorality. First Peter 2:11 says to abstain from sinful desires.

Romans 13:14 tells us, ". . . do not think about how to gratify the desires of the sinful nature." Don't give it a chance to happen! Don't even think about it! For example, **don't go parking or be alone in the dark.** It sounds pretty simple, but if you just stay around a lot of other people and keep the lights on, it is amazing how pure you will stay. It is amazing what you will *not* do if other people are around.

If none of these other reasons have convinced you, do it because God says to. **Even if you don't understand why. Just obey, anyway.** One day you will be walking down the aisle of a church to get married. When you stand there looking your bride or groom in the eyes with no shame, you will be glad you did things God's way.

I remember, just after I was saved, going on a date with a girl who went to a religious school. I was so excited that we could just go out and praise the Lord all night. However, I soon found out that she had other things in mind. When I took her home she began to attack me. I was afraid for my life (at least for my purity). Her lips went into convulsions in my direction. It felt like Jaws was coming towards me! I stopped her and pushed her away long enough to ask, "Wouldn't you rather be reading the Bible right now?"

She said, "No!" and kept coming.

I asked her again and she said, "NO!"

I thought, *This is just great. All my life as a heathen I prayed for this, and it never happened! Now that I'm saved it happens!* So I stopped her again and asked her the same question, "Are you sure you wouldn't rather be reading the Bible right now?"

She said, "No! Why? Would you?"

I replied, "Well, yeah, I would!"

She opened up her door and got out. She slammed it and stomped her way back to her front door.

I drove away excited! I said NO! I said NO! It feels so good to say NO! You can say "no," too. One thing I learned is, DON'T PUT YOURSELF IN A POSITION WHERE THAT KIND OF THING WILL HAPPEN! It is a lot easier to say NO when all the lights are on at McDonald's; in fact, it probably won't even come up in the conversation.

What If You Have Already Blown It?

"All this sounds great, but what if I have already messed up?"

Good news for you. Jesus still forgives! His love will wash away your past as if it had never happened. He will forget it, and He will help you to forget it, too. You must ask Him to forgive you, and then you must repent. Put your foot down and say, "No more!"

Some people think, *Well since I have already blown it, it doesn't matter if I keep messing up.* WRONG! The more you fool around, the more it will mess up your head, your heart, and your marriage! It is time to stop now. It is time to start over again. **It is time to begin your second virginity.**

That's right, I said — second virginity! Now that you know about living pure, you can stay pure from this time forward. You need to put some time between the present and the last time you messed up. The longer you stay clean, the more pure and holy you will feel!

The most important thing about being pure is your heart. God wants you to have what I call, "the spirit of a virgin." Some people have never blown it physically, but they think about it all the time — looking at pornography or lusting after other people. Their body is pure but their heart is not. Those who get married like this are miserable. They do not have "the spirit of a virgin."

On the other hand, there are others who have blown it big time. But they repented, got their heart right, and kept their life pure. They walked down the aisle without any shame because they knew they had "the spirit of a virgin," and now these people have great marriages.

It would be better if we could have a pure body and heart entering into marriage, and it is safer. But as you commit to a second virginity and to keeping your heart pure, you will have everything you need for a great sex life in marriage.

Because My body is the temple of the Holy Spirit, I commit to stay free from any sexual activity, including petting as well as intercourse until the day I get married. Thank You, Jesus, for the power to stay pure and holy every day.

_____
signed

_____
date

6

Missionary Dating: Reaching Someone through Dating

As you know, dating is an issue that just about every teen has on his mind, and everyone has his own opinion of how to go about it. As a Christian, you must first find out what would please God about your dating life before you decide to date anyone.

Some young people get into a romantic relationship with someone who is not even a Christian thinking that somehow God will bless it. The problem is that too many young people are more committed to finding a boyfriend or girlfriend than they are to God. They figure God will understand; and if they get into trouble, He will get them out.

Even as I write this, I know a young lady who loves the Lord, but is too desperate to find a guy. She has been a Christian for years, and has been known as a leader. Everyone respects her and looks up to her. She has been toying with the idea of dating a guy that wants her, for a long time.

He is barely saved, and surely does not live like it. All her friends have talked to her about it, but she refuses to listen to them. She says they are being judgmental and do not really know him. She is using whatever excuse she can to keep thinking she is justified in dating him. The problem is that she wants a boyfriend more than she wants to do what is right. She could be in for some big trouble.

There are three major reasons that come to mind as to why teens date and how they rationalize dating non-Christians.

1. The Thing to Do

In America, it seems like all the TV shows and movies glamorize the teen "love" relationships. Peer pressure makes you feel "stupid and ugly" if you don't date. We have the great American dating game: "you date 'em or you hate 'em." There are hardly any genuine friendships between guys and girls. Often, if you pursue a friendship with a person, he thinks you like him romantically. You get sucked into the subtle pressure that if you don't have a boyfriend or girlfriend, something must be wrong with you. Many times our self–esteem revolves around whether we are dating or not.

As a result, we spend a lot of our time trying to impress the opposite sex, to lure them to our way. Most teens are totally preoccupied with the notion of dating. If you have a boyfriend or girlfriend, that's all you think about. If you don't have one, you think about the one you wish you had. It all revolves around the American myth that if you date you will be happy. But because these kinds of relationships are totally based on insecurity and not maturity, they usually end up with someone's heart getting broken.

Too many people are forced to compromise their Christianity and end up dating *anyone* they can, even a non–Christian, just because they feel the pressure of the American dating game. I know that with all your friends dating, and all the TV shows and movies saying it is cool and fun to date around, it might not be popular to NOT date.

There's another issue to deal with regarding dating: your personal happiness. You look around and see all the dating couples, and it seems like they are very happy just because they have this relationship. What no one seems willing to talk about is this: If you are not happy before you date, you will not be happy when you start to date. In fact, it could be more dangerous! If you start to date, and you do not get happy, then you think, "Maybe it's because I need to get more intimate, or go all the way." So you end up doing what you never wanted to do just trying to get happy, and you never find the happiness you were looking for. Let me save you the trouble — find your happiness in Jesus.

You might not want to hear this, but if your reason for dating is to try to fit into this myth, you are not ready to date. Wait. Let God show you that you are all right the way you are, without a romantic relationship. Only then will you be mature enough to handle a dating relationship. (See chapter 13).

2. Friendship and Fun

Many young people date because they want companionship and someone to hang out with and have fun with. While this may be a valid desire, and a great benefit of a healthy dating relationship, is it a good enough reason to expose your heart and emotions to another?

Many people underestimate the potential of a romantic relationship and the power it has to manipulate feelings and decisions. You may say, "It's not like I'm married, I'm just dating." But the fact is, your whole life begins to revolve around that one relationship.

The fact is, once you start dating someone, you get so caught up in the emotions of the whole thing, that you forget all about real friendships most of the time. Then, if you start kissing, you substitute that for talking. So the thing you wanted, you do not end up with anyway. You think you are close friends because you kiss, but you are still lonely on the inside.

If your reason for dating is for friendships and fun, go

out with groups of your friends and have a blast together! You don't have to expose your emotions to possible major damage (as you would surely do, especially if you are thinking about dating a non–Christian) just to have fun. Go out with a bunch of "buds" you don't have to worry about impressing. Cut loose and enjoy being a teen without having to worry about getting your heart broken.

Don't you dare take the risk of getting your emotions all tangled up with anyone, especially a non–Christian, when what you are really wanting is just to have a good time with friends! God can give you that with a wild group of radicals who love Him!

3. Potential Partner

I'm sure you have heard that the Bible says, "Do not be yoked together with unbelievers . . ." (2 Cor. 6:14). This Scripture is talking about friendships as well as romantic relationships. Definitely the most mature and wholesome dating relationships are between people who are serious about pursuing a lifelong mate, and not just breaking hearts. Whether or not you are dating someone to pursue a marriage relationship, you need to seriously consider this Scripture.

If you read all of Paul's second letter to the Corinthians, you will notice that he was not speaking to those who are young and immature in this Scripture. Our maturity in Christ is not measured by how close we can get to disobeying the Bible and still keep our salvation. Our maturity is measured by how obedient we are to the Scripture even when it is not easy to obey. **How radically committed are you to doing what is right no matter what this world or your friends say?**

"But," you may say, "I am strong enough to date a non–Christian. I have been in church all my life! I am not a baby anymore."

The question is not are *you* strong enough to date a non–Christian, but is *any* Christian strong enough? Is it wise to put yourself in that position? It's like when the devil tempted Jesus to go to the temple and throw himself down saying that

God would catch Him. Jesus said, ". . . Do not put the Lord your God to the test" (Matt. 4:7). Getting involved romantically with a non–Christian is the same test. You are going against God's Word and asking God to bless it, and hoping He will pull you through if something goes wrong.

It's not a matter of whether your faith can endure it or whether you can keep your salvation. We need to do everything we possibly can to grow in God. We must passionately pursue our Saviour with all we've got. We cannot afford to let anything slow us down or distract us. Dating an unbeliever, or someone who is not radically sold out to God, is definitely dead weight.

To be yoked with someone means that you begin to get your hearts twined together. You begin to share special moments together and talk about deep issues from your heart. Now, if you attempt this with an unbeliever, how can you share a common heart if you don't have the same thing in your hearts — namely, Jesus? How can you pursue any type of meaningful relationship if you look at life from completely different perspectives? You have Jesus as the center of your life and he has something else.

Many people try to "missionary date" and bring their dates to the Lord. Let me tell you, there are too many tragic endings to that story. Many on–fire young people who had good intentions end up trashing their relationship with God and even completely turning their back on Him. They "fall in love," at least what the world calls love, and they forget about their **first love** (Rev. 2:4). They end up in a relationship, and even a marriage, that is lonely and unwhole because God is not in the middle of it.

Another girl in my youth group really loved the Lord. Her heart's desire was to someday be involved in the ministry full-time with her husband. After dating several guys as a teen (they were sort-of-saved), she got more serious with a guy who seemed nice enough, but did not have a passionate heart after God. He went to youth group, but it was clear he had no intention of being in full-time ministry.

She did not think much about it because she thought, *Surely this would not end up in marriage.*

It turns out they got more serious, and he did ask her to marry her. She was swept off her feet and forgot the lifelong dream of her heart, to be in the ministry. I counseled her right before the wedding that she would be sorry because she would be compromising her dreams and always regret it. She felt it was too close to the wedding to call it off (it's never too close if it is NOT RIGHT) so she went through with it.

She told me later, "I knew within a week that I should have done what you said." Soon her husband got into pornography, and wanted her to watch it with him. She went through years of pain and frustration, and finally he is serving the Lord wholeheartedly. Still, she will always live with the regret of missing her calling and not being in the ministry full-time. She gave up her lifelong dream for a guy that could never live up to what she always wanted.

If the person you're thinking about is not a Christian, then the last thing he needs is for you to date him. He needs to be thinking about eternity and his relationship with God, not about gooey feelings for you. **You could actually keep him from having a relationship with God** because he is infatuated with you instead of getting serious about God. If you really love him with God's love, stay out of his emotions until he has a sold–out, fired–up, turned–on relationship with the Father!

This is not something to take lightly. The devil could use a relationship with an unbeliever to totally mess up your relationship with the Lord. This is a matter of life and death spiritually. Don't take a chance! Don't play with fire; you will surely get burned, and the pain could last the rest of your life.

Do it God's way. It is always the best. He will totally blow you away with blessing your face off if you stay radically committed to His Word and only pursue wholesome relationships with someone sold out to Him.

7

God's Love Connection: A Radical Dating Agenda

Teenage romantic involvement is where many a world changer has been buried in the graveyard of unfulfilled potential. They were going for God really well until someone distracted them and they got sucked into something that they could never get out of.

Why do most teens date? These are some of the reasons that teens have given us:

— They find themselves in confusion so they get involved with someone who will help them. That is why relationships don't work, because they are both confused and they end up doing things that are crazy.

— To find out what kind of mate they want to marry, what kind of man or woman of God they want.

— Insecurities, to find themselves a relationship.

— They are looking for security, for someone to love and accept them and to be with them. So they look for it in the opposite sex.

— It is a cultural thing; the culture tells them they have to date.

— They are insecure and are looking for something and they don't know what it is. They think that companionship and being with someone is what they need, but it is not.

Supposedly, young people are trying to find "LOVE" as they pursue dating relationships. The word "LOVE" is thrown around so much these days it is hard to know what it really is. We say we "LOVE" pizza, or that we "LOVE" the weather today. So when we say we "LOVE" a person, it ranks right up there with pizza?

What is love? We asked a bunch of teens what they thought love is:

— The way God loves you and cares for you, He wants you to be with Him.

— Caring about someone and knowing him, his being your best friend, having total trust in him, he will not lie to you, he will do anything for you, having respect for him, giving your heart to him, and feeling comfortable with him.

— God is love. He sets the best example through Jesus in the Bible.

— When you feel someone is special to you.

— Knowing someone completely — the good and the bad — and still being able to accept him for who he is and where he is.

— Not a feeling, something in you that God put in you, and I don't know how to explain it very well.

One of the first commandments in the Bible is God saying, ". . . Be fruitful and increase in number; fill the earth . . ." (Gen. 1:28). So we know God is totally into romance, and even into the intimacy of sex. You notice Adam and Eve did not disobey this command. Imagine Adam's face after God told him what He wanted them to do. I'm sure he thought, *Bummer, Dude, but I guess I better obey the Lord!*

1. Small-time Love

This is what I call most of what happens in romantic relationships. We think what we see on TV and among our friends is so awesome, but really it is a cheap substitute for the real thing. We see small–time love in action almost everywhere we look.

A. America's preoccupation with love, sex, and dating; TV game shows, soaps, and serials; magazines and books. All small-time love.

B. Teens' preoccupation with boyfriends and girlfriends, love, dating, sex. Most of them result in broken hearts at the very least, lost purity and unwanted pregnancies far too often. Small-time love.

C. The most romantic movies or scenarios possible. Small-time love.

Even Christians who date get their priorities messed up, get distracted, and settle for a mediocre walk with God. Here's a checklist to gauge your romantic relationships.

— How much time do you spend thinking about your friend?

— Do you have any other close friendships?

— What if you didn't have each other? Would you be devastated? Do you not even want to think about it?

— Is it hard to pray and read your Bible together?

— Do you substitute time with each other for time with God?

— Did you have a more intimate walk with God before you dated?

If any of these questions make you angry or uncomfortable, you could be on a path of destruction for your heart, life, and walk with God.

2. Big-time Love

In the beginning, God made the earth, stars, plants, and sun; then He made all the animals. Everything He did was GOOD, the Bible says. Everything He did was excellent, but something was missing. God had a problem.

The Bible says in I John 4:16, ". . . God is love. . . ." He doesn't just *have* love, He is *made* of the stuff. It's His nature. He loves without even thinking about it. It's all He knows how to do and all He wants to do. You can't get close to God without getting loved.

The problem is this: LOVE NEEDS TO GIVE. LOVE

NEEDS TO LOVE. God needed someone to give to, someone to love who could really receive His love. He needed someone who was built to handle His love and who could really enjoy it and appreciate it. None of the animals and plants were made of the right stuff to appreciate the awesomeness of His love.

He wanted someone who could fully experience what it was like to really be loved by the Author of Love, and who could reciprocate that love if he chose to.

So, God decided He would make someone for the sole purpose of receiving His love. All the plants and animals He either spoke into existence or made from the ground. But in order to make sure this new creation could fully appreciate His love, He said, ". . . Let us make man in our image . . ." (Gen. 1:26). In other words, in order for him to understand love, Love (God) had to go back to himself and make something out of himself (love) so that the new creation could receive and reciprocate His love.

Apparently God made Adam and Eve for one reason: to be the object of His love. He made all of mankind so that all the power of His love could be aimed at us. You are the object of His love. You've got a bull's–eye painted on you, and His love is the arrow.

Some have said we were created to have fellowship with God, or to glorify God, or to dominate the earth. But the original reason is that God had so much love, He couldn't keep it to himself. He had to give it, so He made you and me with the express purpose and ability to receive His love.

No wonder the Bible says things like:

> Keep me as the apple of your eye . . . (Ps. 17:8).
> If I go up to the heavens, you are there; if I make my bed in the depths, you are there (Ps. 139:8).
> . . . Nor anything . . . will be able to separate us from the love of God . . . (Rom. 8:39).

You can't really know love until you know God.

Nothing you've done — no sin, no problem — can keep His love away. It doesn't matter how fast you run, His love will run faster. You can't find a place where His love wouldn't go to get you. His love is in relentless pursuit of YOU.

God has a love affair going on with you. He has a connection, a love connection, with the world and He will not let go.

When you realize the purpose for which you were made, you don't need a boyfriend or girlfriend to make you feel loved or important. The Creator of love made you to love.

When you have the revelation, "GOD LOVES ME!" nothing else really matters. You don't need someone like you thought you did. You need the real thing — BIG-TIME LOVE — from GOD.

Adam hung out with God and just enjoyed getting blasted with His love every day. He was busy doing what God told him to do — naming the animals and tending the garden. He didn't look for a girlfriend or a wife. God is the one Who said, ". . . It's not good for the man to be alone . . ." (Gen. 2:18). The Bible says He brought the woman to Adam; Adam didn't have to go looking for her (Gen. 2:22).

In the same way, you don't have to hunt for love like other teens are doing. Adam was so blown away by being God's target for love, he didn't need or want anything else. The very first love affair was not between Adam and Eve, it was between Adam and God. This was the first LOVE CONNECTION.

3. Ready for Some Real Love?

A. Do Something Wild

Is it possible after reading this information that you could be sucked into a relationship? Could you still get a broken heart? Get into immorality? Get pregnant? You bet it is!

I don't want one person to lose his or her virginity after having read this. I don't want one to get pregnant or get someone pregnant before marriage. I don't want one who has been sexually active in the past to do it again until marriage.

This is not possible unless we make a wild commitment. A commitment that goes against the grain of teenage America. Are you ready?

B. Commit To A Love Affair With God

Stay away from the games of even Christian dating long enough to really see things clearly. If you think you need a boyfriend or girlfriend, then you're not ready for a relationship.

Let your life become radically GOD–centered for an entire year, then let God bring you a person just like He did with Adam.

Date God for a year. Until you've dated God for a year, you aren't ready to date a person. Let Him blast you with His love for a full year with no distractions.

Guys, commit to treat the ladies ". . . as sisters, with absolute purity" (1 Tim. 5:2), especially for this next year. Ladies, commit to not date, flirt with, or even hope for a guy for the next year.

The time you would have spent with your boyfriend or girlfriend, spend with God. Instead of talking with your friend, talk to God and pray. Instead of writing love notes, write in your journal what God is doing in your life. Instead of going out on a date, go on a fast or pray all night. Instead of thinking about someone of the opposite sex, meditate on the Word. Instead of making plans to be with someone, make plans to change the world with God! You don't think it's possible? Read on!!

I was on a plane sitting next to a young lady and we began to talk. She told me that she was a Christian and had been living for the Lord for a long time. She was now in college and she told me that she was dating her first guy. Now let me be honest with you, this was not an ugly girl. I said, "Wait a minute. You are telling me that all through high school you never went on a date?"

She replied, "Nope."

I said, "Why?"

She answered, "My dad wouldn't let me."

I said, "Did you have a boyfriend anyway, like at school? Or did you ever sneak out at night?"

She said "No."

Wow, I could not believe it. I asked her why he had that rule. She said it started as a joke, "You are not going to date until you're 25." The joke kept going on, and on, and on.

I asked her if she hated her dad. She said that she didn't, and that their commitment had protected her from all the broken hearts that she saw all of her friends having to work through over and over. She went on, "I had a bunch of great friends all through high school. The guys knew I couldn't date, so they never asked me out. It was like I had a bunch of guys who were my friends or brothers. The girls knew I couldn't date so they were never wondering if I would steal their boyfriends."

I asked her if she felt like she really missed out on a lot in high school because she did not date. She said, "Every time a girl friend of mine broke up, she would come crying to me with her broken heart. I never had to go through that."

She was, at the time I talked to her, engaged to marry the first guy she had ever dated or kissed and was so glad she had saved her heart only for him.

"Sure, that is great for the girls," you might be saying if you are a guy, "but what about us men? Real men have to date around, don't they?"

I talked with a guy in Florida a few years ago. He was a cool–looking guy who surfed a lot. He loved the Lord and was serving Him with all his heart. I asked him about his girlfriend. He said he did not have one. I said "Come on, I'm sure you have girls coming after you all the time. Why don't you date?"

He said that he made a commitment not to date when he was 13. He remembered seeing a lot of his friends come to youth group and then start dating. He said, "It seemed like every time they began dating, even if they were dating someone who was a Christian, they started coming less and less to church. Every single person started falling away from God, and some have never come back."

Then he looked me in the eye and said, "I NEVER WANTED TO TAKE THE CHANCE OF THAT HAPPENING TO ME!"

Wow! That is pretty radical. I believe that God is looking for many more radicals who so strongly would not even want to take a CHANCE of falling away from Him that they just chill out on the dating scene.

Some of you have been looking for love from a boyfriend or girlfriend for a long time. You've got to get it from the Author of Love. You need to experience the Original Love Affair.

MAKE A LOVE CONNECTION AND A COMMITMENT WITH GOD TODAY.

Certificate of Courtship

I hereby commit my emotions, time, will, and body in seeking God and developing an intense love affair with Him for an entire year starting on

_____.

I will not seek to entice, flirt, or lead anyone on. I will in no way initiate a romantic relationship with anyone. I don't need another. I'm in a true love affair with God.

_____

(signature)

_____

(date)

8

Dancing: Time to Change Partners

After all that we have already talked about concerning relationships, I cannot imagine someone still asking, "Is it okay to go to a dance?" Since we as Christians should be getting as far away as we can from anything that even resembles the world's idea of romance, it is probably not a good idea. But far be it from me to ask someone to do something without explaining why, so here it goes.

The word dance means: to move the body and feet to rhythm, ordinarily to music. The idea is that you move your body to the beat of whatever you are listening to. If you are listening to secular music, then you are moving your body as someone is expressing his ideas about life without God. We know the fruit of listening to secular music (see chapter 16). You might say, "Does that mean we cannot even listen to secular music at a dance?"

Well, are you going to decide to keep as pure as humanly possible or not? So, say you go to a secular dance (a normal, public school dance). Not only are you getting that garbage (the music) in your brain, you begin to move your body to it. You let the beat of a song that talks about heathen attitudes and lifestyles dictate how and when you will move your body? This is the most graphic form of letting the music tell you what to do.

Rave dances are the thing that some teens are into lately. I went and watched a rave club for teens recently. The music was blasting (like it was trying to drown out every thought in your head). The teens on the dance floor looked like they were dancing with themselves. Their eyes were shut and they did not even know if their dance partner was still on the floor with them. It is like they were shutting out the rest of the world trying to believe everything was okay. A bunch of lonely young people all hanging out in one group.

In a way you are celebrating the music when you dance. You are letting it get you excited and cause you to move.

The next point is that most of the time, when dancing with a partner at a school dance, there are romantic or sexual overtones in the music and the dances. Let's get real. People are there to pick up on each other. They want to score. They want to hook onto you like a blood–sucking leach and hang on as long as they can. It is the American dating game at its best.

You might say, "But that is not why I go, I just want to have fun." Maybe your way of fun is flirting at a dance and acting like you did not know you were doing it? Is it fun to get the attention of leading others on, and then just let them down? Maybe you do not have bad motives, but others do. You expose yourself to an unnecessary game and risk.

The Bible speaks about dancing to the Lord. "You turned my wailing into dancing . . ." (Ps. 30:11). David danced before the ark of the covenant (2 Sam. 6:16). The idea here is that they were excited about what God was doing, and out of that excitement they began to move their body. If you are going to move your body in a wild, rhythmic way, it might as well be about something that is worth going crazy for.

Every once in a while I walk by a bar with a window, and I look inside to watch the people dancing. Have you ever really looked at those people doing their thing? They look incredibly stupid, but they don't even know it. They think they are so cool as they move their bodies in the most ridiculous ways. I usually leave laughing my head off. I can't believe that people would move their bodies in public like they do. And they call us Christians weird?? They need to look in the mirror while they dance!

We can see a great example of people getting really excited in Exodus. God had just opened up the Red Sea, the Israelites had crossed over, and now all of Pharaoh's army had just drowned. God had rescued them! It was a miracle! They were so psyched up they cranked up the tunes! (i.e. they sang and hit the tambourine and possibly drums). They could not contain their excitement! They had to move their bodies. The Bible says that Miriam (Moses' sister) ". . . took a tambourine in her hand, and all the women followed her, with tambourines and dancing" (Exod. 15:20). Now they had a reason to dance.

The next time you hear about dancing is when some of the same people were dancing in front of the golden calf they had made (Exod. 32:6-19). They were not excited about the Lord any more, so they made an idol. Sometimes I think Christians are the same way. They do not *feel* close to God anymore, so they find something else to get psyched up about. They find an idol to get happy about (secular music sings about a lot of modern day idols). Then they move their body and dance to their idol, just like the Israelites did!

Moses saw what they were doing and he got really steamed at them. In fact, he got so mad he threw down the stone tablets of the Ten Commandments God had written out for him, and he broke them. I wonder if God has that attitude today with Christians who rejoice to anything except Him?

Dancing in Sync

Many young people are into dancing in sync to hip-hop tunes, like a routine. It seems to me that as long as this is done to Christian music, then it would be okay. The reason I feel that this is acceptable is that most of the time these routines are learned to be performed as a ministry tool, so there is not even a hint of romantic involvement.

"What about a Christian dance, where they play Christian music?" Is there such a thing? I have heard of people try to pull it off. I think it is just a cheap imitation of what the world is doing. They try to pretend it is godly, but the same attitudes of romantic and sexual enticement are present. They try to justify it because they are moving their bodies to Christian music. This is even worse than a secular dance. Trying to schmooze people into thinking that it is okay to be worldly just because you are using Christian tunes makes me want to throw up!

"But can't we teens who love God have any fun?" NO!

I'm just kidding! Of course, you can have fun, but you do not have to imitate the world just so you can look them in the eyes and say, "See, we can have fun just like you do!" You can have a ripping blast with a bunch of fired-up radical friends like I described in earlier chapters. Go out as a group. Have fun! Go on an adventure together. Just do everything you can to make sure you stay pure and holy. You do not have to imitate the world to have fun. God invented fun. So when you have fun God's way, you don't get the second-class thing, you get the real thing!

Section III

Who's in the House? The "Fam Thing"

I have talked to teenagers all over North America who are trying with all their hearts to follow the Lord. One of the topics that I constantly hear about is their families.

They tell me how they really want to serve the Lord, but their mom and dad are not saved. Or they are saved, but they do not live what they preach. So many teens have been disillusioned about their whole Christian life because of what they have seen in their parents.

It is hard to keep believing that God is going to help out your family, when both your mom and dad are Christians and yet they are both wanting a divorce. I have seen it over and over. Others have told me of the intense circumstances in their homes with their parents or stepparents. "How do I deal with my mom who is an alcoholic?" or "What should I do about my dad who is a pastor, but he sexually abuses me?"

These next few chapters are to help you as a teen, or as a parent, to gain some godly responses to some of the most intense predicaments I have seen. If you are a teen, do not judge the goodness of God based only on what you see from your parents. He is bigger than that. Whatever situation you are facing right now, I am confident that He will help you just as I know He helped me get through them. Just hang on to Him!

9

How to Get Your Parents to Let You Do Whatever You Want to Do

Teens everywhere are constantly wishing they had more freedom. They want their parents to allow them to do more. The desire for responsibility is a good thing, but sometimes it turns into rebellion when you don't think you're getting it quickly enough. When your parents see rebellion in you, they do the exact opposite of what you want them to do: They clamp down.

To get your parents to let you do what you want, you must honor them.

1. Why Honor Them?

A. It's God's plan from the beginning.

God created Adam and Eve and told them to ". . . Rule over the fish of the sea and the birds of the air and over every living creature that moves on the ground" (Gen. 1:28). That included their kids. God put the parents, not the kids, in charge of the family.

Imagine what it would have been like if Cain and Abel were in charge in the beginning!

A lot of the problems in our homes today (even Christian homes) have to do with the fact that kids run the house in many ways. They boss their parents around or manipulate them in other ways. When this happens, the order of how things should be run gets reversed. The results are confusion and tension in the family.

Let's say, for example, Susie asks mom if she can go to the ball game on Friday night. Mom says, "No, you got a bad grade on your history test this week, you need to stay home and study."

So Susie goes to ask Dad and he says, "You are my little girl, of course you can go."

Mom walks by Susie's room on Friday night as she gets ready to go and she says, "I thought I told you that you couldn't go." Susie responds, "Dad said I could." Mom goes to talk to Dad about it, and a fight explodes as Susie is walking out the door.

This is a simple example of how teens manipulate their parents to get their own way. They create confusion and tension in the home and then wonder why they don't ever want to just hang around the house. There are a lot of other ways of trying to manipulate Mom and Dad; from whining, to crying, to threatening, to being openly rebellious. I know that not all the tension in a home is created by the teen, but surely some can be avoided by treating our parents with respect.

Romans 13:1–2 says, "Everyone must submit himself to the governing authorities, for there is no authority except that which God has established. The authorities that exist have been established by God. Consequently, he who rebels against the authority is rebelling against what God has instituted, and those who do so will bring judgment on themselves."

If you ever have wondered why things don't seem to be going right in your life, check to see if you are bringing judgment on yourself by not honoring your parents.

It's like Adam and Eve were the king and queen over the earth. They were to raise princes and princesses on the earth who would:

> be responsible,
> be smart,
> know how to think,
> be sober,
> be obedient to God,
> make wise decisions,
> be able to govern and lead others, and
> have a broad perspective on life.

Your parents have the same mandate: to raise you as a prince or princess, ready to govern skillfully when you are of age. God gave them this responsibility. That is why it is so important to honor your parents.

B. There are great advantages to honoring you parents.

Ephesians 6:2–3 says, " 'Honour your father and mother' — which is the first commandment with a promise — 'that it may go well with you and that you may enjoy long life on the earth.' "

God promises that if you honor your parents, He will blow you away by blessing your life for a long, long time. The blessing and favor of the Lord are on your side when you honor them. You can be sure you are on the right track to fulfilling all your potential if you stay submissive to the authority that God gave your parents.

2. How to Honor Your Parents

A. Honor your parents by listening to them.

Proverbs 1:5 says, "Let the wise listen and add to their learning." Do you really want to be smart? Listen to your mom and dad. I know it's a novel concept, but just try it. It's amazing how many mistakes it will keep you from making. Don't just do it because you're supposed to, do it to really find out where they are coming from. Ask them questions so you can get their perspective. Ask, "Why?" a lot, but not with an attitude. Get their views of why they have particular rules for you, or why they don't want you to do something. Find out the reasons for their rules, and you'll be a lot smarter than if you obey just because you're told to.

As you learn from your parents by listening to them, the things you want to do will probably change because you've become smarter.

B. Honor your parents in the way you speak to them.

So many teens bring shame on themselves by the way they talk to or about their parents. The Bible says in Ephesians 4:29, "Do not let any unwholesome talk come out of your mouths. . . ." This is hardly the case with most teens concerning their parents. Maybe it's murmuring under your breath after they tell you to do something or outright bursts of anger toward them.

I remember once, when I was 16, my dad and I were in a fight about my car. I wanted to take it, and he said, "No." He had my keys in his pocket. I said, "Give me those keys, or I will tackle you and do whatever I have to do to get them." I was a little bigger than my dad at the time so he gave me the keys. I have regretted those words for a long time. Instead of respecting the authority God had given my dad, I humiliated him.

Many parents have been hurt by things their kids have said. Even if your parents aren't (in your opinion) doing the best job in the world, they gave you life. They brought you into this world.

An overwhelming majority of teens say they lie to their parents. *Is this honoring them?* Honor your parents by what you say.

C. Honor your parents by obeying them.

Ephesians 6:1 says, "Children, obey your parents in the Lord, for this is right." I know this doesn't sound like a vacation. It sounds like slavery to a lot of teens. But this is God's way of doing things.

Colossians 3:22 says, "Slaves, obey your earthly masters in everything; and do it, not only when their eye is on you and to win their favour, but with sincerity of heart and reverence for the Lord."

Go overboard, bend over backwards to obey your parents. Not just their commands, but their desires as well. Don't try to just get by. Don't try to get away with things.

Find out what they really want done, and do it. Go for the spirit of the law and not just the letter of the law. Find out their whims and wishes. Then blow them away by doing what they want.

Obey your parents even when you don't agree with them — especially when you don't want to. That's your chance to prove you are submitting to their God–given authority, and this pleases God.

The more willingly you submit and obey from your heart, the more open your parents will be to letting you have more freedom.

D. Honor your parents by showing responsibility.

Many teens want the opportunity to make their own decisions but have not really shown they are responsible enough to do so. Jesus told the parable of the talents in Matthew 25. The master commended his servants saying, ". . . You have been faithful with a few things; I will put you in charge of many things . . ." (Matt. 25:21). If you want to have more responsibility, you must show that you are awesome at handling the little you have now.

How do you spend your free time? How about your money? How fast do you drive? Any traffic tickets? These are all signs to your mom and dad. If you don't prove faithful in the small things, they will never give you more of what you want.

Don't always try to take a free ride. Try to pay for your own stuff once in a while instead of asking them for money all the time. When you are in the wrong, 'fess up to it. Admit your mistakes and ask them to forgive you. When you do this, you are taking responsibility for your actions.

I remember doing something wrong on purpose after I

was saved. I did it just so I could admit it and be responsible and take punishment. My dad never said anything to me about it. Two days later I asked, "Dad, did you know I was out all night a couple of nights ago?"

He said, "Yes."

I said, "Dad, did you know that the Bible says that a man who doesn't discipline his son hates his son? Dad, do you hate me?"

He responded, "I think you're starting to grow up, Son."

> He who spares the rod hates his son, but he who loves him is careful to discipline him (Prov. 13:24).

It's good to desire more responsibility, but don't let your desire for it turn into rebellion. If you start thinking, *I'm old enough, I'm gonna do it anyway,* you immediately get OUT OF GOD'S BLESSING, and your life will get really messed up.

As you prove your responsibility and honor your parents, God will open the doors for you to do the things that He wants you to do. After all, if He doesn't want you to do it, it can't be that great!

Stop right now and take some time to ask God to forgive you for any way you may have dishonored your parents. Think about what you have just read. Think of each specific situation when you were disrespectful to them, and ask God to forgive you. Make a commitment to God to honor your parents with all your heart. You may even want to go and talk to your parents about it. Ask them to forgive you. It does not matter if they have made a mistake; do not expect them to ask you to forgive them. You do it first. You will be amazed at what will happen in your relationship with your parents when you begin to honor them.

10

Dealing with Unsaved or Ungodly Parents

As I travel all over North America speaking to thousands of teenagers each week, one of the most heartbreaking situations I hear about is how these Christian young people are being treated by their parents. Some have parents who call themselves Christians but hardly reflect that in the way they treat their kids. Others have parents who are not Christians and do not understand what their kids have gotten into. It seems that one of the toughest plights a young person faces is that once he really decides to serve God, he faces daily persecution and intimidation from unbelieving or ungodly parents.

I talked to one teenage guy a few weeks ago who was crying his eyes out trying to forgive his parents. He asked me what he should do about his mom, who constantly drank and was hardly ever sober. He wanted to serve the Lord with all his heart, but she was making it really hard for him to even survive.

Sometimes parents get mad when their kids get really

committed to Jesus and want to live a righteous life. They might have a teen who's been drinking and really messing up, and they don't say much to him. But as soon as they get turned on to the Lord they go crazy and start harassing them and making fun of them. Even my own dad did that to me as a teen. I found out through a third party that he was calling me a "Jesus freak" and acting like I had gone off the deep end after I got saved. I don't know if it is because they think their kids have actually joined a cult, or if it is because they feel guilty because their kids want to live more pure than they did or do right now.

I talked to one girl who went on a mission trip with Teen Mania a few years ago. While she was gone, her parents decided to surprise her. They stood in line at 4 a.m. to buy her tickets to a secular concert that was coming to town when she got home. When she returned they told her about the tickets, and she told them that she didn't want to go because she didn't want that kind of influence in her life.

They were irate! They got so mad that they had gone out of their way to get these tickets for her, and now she "loved God" too much to go. They didn't look at the principle, they just got mad — and they were "Christian" parents.

Our purpose here is not to judge whether or not parents are Christians. Only God can judge their heart. While some openly admit they are not, others claim they are believers. We need to find out how to respond to them whatever the circumstances in the home may be.

Why Obey?

Parents all over the world have one thing in common. Any parent who has ever heard of the Bible has one favorite verse, and he is careful to make sure his children learn it. It is Ephesians 6:1–2: "Children, obey your parents in the Lord, for this is right. 'Honour your father and mother. . . .' " Even parents who do not know anything about the Bible seem to know this verse, and they love to use it to try to force their kids to honor and obey them.

Let us examine these verses a little more closely. They

say children are to obey their parents. The word "parent" means "to produce." When you *parent* something, your goal is to produce something that will be strong and healthy. It is like a garden. When you plant a garden, your goal is to tend it, or take care of it, until it produces a healthy crop. In order to do that, you must water and fertilize your plants.

That is exactly what parents must do to help their teens grow up to be mature and wise. Parents must water and fertilize — they should be pouring into you the ingredients you need to succeed in life. Sometimes they have to pull weeds in your life (i.e. not let you do the things you want to do). The Bible says that when we find these people who are pouring into us like this, we should obey them with all our hearts — **they are looking out for our best interests**. That is why some young people find it easier to obey an aunt or grandparent than they do their parents. They get the feeling they are being watered and fertilized by others more than by their own parents.

Does this mean we should blindly obey every whim of our parents, even if it is not scriptural? Let's talk about the concept of honoring them.

Honoring When It Is Hard

You may be in a situation where it is extremely difficult to honor your mom and dad. Honoring is different from obeying. Just because you took out the garbage when you were told does not mean that you honored your parents. If you did it with a bad attitude, you gave them no honor. Some people think that if their parents are really mean to them, then they do not have to honor them. The truth is, honoring your parents has nothing to do with the way they treat you.

We honor our parents because of their position, not because of what they have done, good or bad. For example, we honor the president because of his position. You might not like his policies, his philosophy, or the way he does his hair. But, he *is* the president of the United States, and you honor him because of that.

The same principle is true regarding your parents. You

may not like their rules, their philosophies, or the clothes they wear, but they *are* your parents. God gave them that position. Of all the people in the world, He chose those two to bring you into the world. He could have chosen anyone else, but He chose them. No one can take that position away from them. No matter what bad or good things they have done, God made them your parents. He wants you to honor them.

When you honor your parents, people will look at you and say, "Wow, you must have had great parents!" That brings honor to them. Your life points to them and people think your parents are awesome, even if they have never met them.

So, what is the difference between honoring and obeying them? Sometimes to honor them you cannot do the specific thing they ask you to do. For example, if your parents asked you to do something illegal or immoral, that would not bring them honor for you to do that thing. People, if they found out, would think, *What terrible parents yours must have been to raise you like this.* God gave you a conscience for a reason. He wants you to follow what you know is right. If I would have "obeyed" my parents to the fullest extent, I never would have moved away and gone to an expensive Christian college. Of course, now people look at me and say, "What great parents you had!" The truth is, neither one of them was a Christian, and both would have preferred that I stay home and go to a secular school. If I had "obeyed" them, I would not have brought them honor like I do now.

Does this mean that whenever I want, I do not have to obey them? Not at all! Does it mean that if my parents are not Christians, I do not have to obey them? Not at all! Most of the disagreements that we have with our parents have nothing to do with whether something is scriptural or not. It has to do with whether we would *prefer* to do something or not.

The general rule would be to obey them no matter what.

If indeed you think you have a biblical reason to not obey (e.g., what they are asking is blatantly against the Bible), then you need to talk to your pastor about it before you make any decision. Talk to your youth pastor or others in leadership before you make any drastic moves. Talk to several people whose godly lives you want to imitate. They can help you talk to your parents about it. Find out *why* they want you to do what they are asking. See how you can obey the spirit of their rules if not the letter. (Read the first chapter of Daniel about how to talk to your parents.) The point is, you want to have other people backing you up so that you are not all alone, going against your parent's wishes just because you are rebellious.

Verbal Abuse

Maybe you are in a situation where you are constantly being ripped to shreds by what your parents say to you. So many parents these days say things that just cut the heart right out of their teen, and they do not even realize what they are doing.

Many times, even parents who say they are following the Lord end up saying things that totally tear at the self-esteem of a young person. We have done polls on thousands of teens and found that the things they have been most discouraged by have often come from parents. It is easy to feel completely paralyzed and demoralized by the hurtful things your parents say to you.

I remember thinking as I grew up that I would probably never make it in life. I thought, *If my parents are saying these things to me, and they are supposed to love me the most, I guess I really am a loser.* I remember feeling the pain of words that I heard from them cut my sense of self-worth down to worthlessness. I remember wanting to end my own life after hearing things my parents said to me.

If you are right in the middle of a situation like this, you need to remember that you have a Heavenly Father. He only says good things about you (see chapter 14). He is there to lift you up when you think no one else is. He knows exactly how low you feel and the pain you feel inside. I know it will seem almost impossible for you to hang on, but reach out to Him with all your heart in these times. Escape with your Bible, and let your Father in heaven pick you back up and help you carry on.

Distant Fathers

There are many teens who feel very far away from their fathers. Obviously, if your parents divorce and your father moves out, you are going to feel somewhat farther away from him. This only increases if you never hear from him or if he re-marries. If your mom re-marries, then your father feels strange coming around with the new man there; or he feels like you have a father figure now, and you do not need him anymore.

Some feel distant because their father left when they were very young and they never met him. Others still have both parents living at home yet feel so far away from their dad. He spends so much time reading the paper or watching sports that they never really talk.

I have prayed with thousands of young men who wish that they had a godly father in their life. Each week as I speak at Acquire the Fire conventions, I see hundreds of teenage guys crying their faces off because their dad has let them down. They feel so far away from their dad, like they do not even know them. Most guys don't want to get mushy and say "I wish my dad would say 'I love you' to me," but this really is the heart of the matter. It is okay to want that in your life. God used a male and a female to make you, and you need both of them to love you and to show it in order to be whole.

I have met a lot of teenage guys who were crying out for a close relationship with their dad. They wished so much that their father would just give them a huge bear hug. But we "men" are not supposed to talk about that kind of stuff or those kinds of emotions, so we act like it does not bother us at all.

I have talked to many teenage girls who wish they were close to their dad. As a result of his absence (emotional or physical), they desperately seek attention from other males. Usually, they get the wrong kind of attention. We see a lot of teenage girls dressing however they have to in order to catch the eye of a guy. Too often they end up doing whatever they feel is necessary just to get a guy to "love" them, even to the point of giving away their purity and their dignity.

I talked to one young lady who was just getting ready to graduate from high school. She had invited her dad, who had divorced her mom when she was little. She had not seen him in about 10 years, but he came to her graduation. A few months later she talked with him on the phone and was telling him what was going on in her life. He said, "I am so proud of you."

The girl stopped and said, "Dad, I have waited 18 years to hear those words out of your mouth."

We should not have to wait that long to get affirmation from our dads! If you are a teenage girl trying to get the attention of the guys, let me tell you something: You don't need that kind of love, darling. You need the kind of acceptance that only a father can give you. You will NEVER find it trying to look cute for a guy and giving yourself to him. If you cannot get it from your father, then your Heavenly Father will be glad to give it to you.

In fact, whether you are a guy or a girl, He says He would be "A father to the fatherless . . ." (Ps. 68:5). So if your father is gone out of your life, or if he lives at home but you feel far away from him, God will be your Father. He promised He would. You get the best. He will not leave you hanging. You just need to call out to Him right now and ask Him to be a Father to you. I know it sounds trite, even a little cheesy, but if you need a father, the truth is that He is there for you.

Other Injustices

In a world rampant with families falling apart, it is becoming more and more apparent that the young people of today have been given the short end of the stick. This is not to try to get you to feel sorry for yourself or to get other people to feel sorry for you; it is just a fact. An injustice, according to the dictionary, is a violation of a person's rights. You have a right as a member of the human race to have two parents in your home. It is not asking or hoping for too much to desire a stable home life.

God hates injustice (Prov. 29:27). He hates to see people get ripped off. The fact is: He does not control the *will* of your parents. As a result, many teens get ripped off.

Some teenagers have "Christian" parents acting in a very non–Christian way or just living a life that looks totally hypocritical. They cannot understand why, if God's blessing is supposedly on their life, everything is so messed up? Doesn't this Christianity thing really work? Listen, please do not blame God for your parent's failures. It is not His fault they did not do things His way. Don't let it push you away from God. He did not want it to happen to you this way. This is the time when you should reach out to Him more than ever. This is the time when you need Him to help make sense out of life.

Other young people have a parent who is an alcoholic, and they do not know what to do about it. I have talked to some teens whose parent has a live–in boyfriend or girl-friend. Some have been physically abused by their parent's lover or even by their parent.

I have talked with some teens whose parents are clearly anti–Christian, and they are receiving persecution from them. Some parents hassle their kids more now that they live for God than they did when the kids were on drugs. Some of you have parents who will use your Christianity against you by saying, "I thought you were a Christian!" every time you make a mistake. Some will mock your commitment to Jesus, while still others will punish you by not letting you go to church or youth group because they know you like it so much.

I want to let you know that in spite of all these obstacles, you can overcome! Your parents are not the enemy, Satan is. It is time to stand strong for Jesus no matter what the situation is where you live. This is not to downplay the intensity of the situation you may be in right now. Jesus knows exactly what you are going through. He will meet you right there and help you to be strong!

Finding Christian Parents

As I said earlier, a parent is someone who nurtures you and helps you to grow and mature. If your parents are not Christians, God will give you surrogate Christian parents if you ask Him for them. These are people who can provide the role model and godly advice you need to become a man or woman of God. You just need to ask God to provide them, and then begin looking for them among the people at your church. Ask your pastor or youth pastor to help you find them.

Remember this: While you are looking, or even when you find them, this does not give you an excuse to be openly rebellious to your biological parents. Do not use your Christianity as an excuse not to obey. Do not EVER say, "Well, you are not a Christian. I don't have to obey you." Or, "I can do what I want since you are not saved anyway." Whatever you do, you want to be an example to your parents of what a good Christian is really like.

Jesus said, ". . . let your light shine before men, that they may see your good deeds and praise your Father in heaven" (Matt. 5:16). Let your parents see the living God in your life. Keep going after Him with all your heart. If you are facing tough times at home, tell your leadership at church so they can pray with you about it. Don't just try to do it by yourself. God is going to help you in a big way to make it through your teen years.

11

Divorce, Single Parents, and the Stepparent

Divorce happens so often that people today think it is a normal part of life. People act as if you have a real problem if you cannot get over a divorce. When I was a kid, it was very abnormal, even embarrassing, if your parents were getting a divorce. Now it seems like just a regular part of life.

Society likes to tell us that there are just different kinds of families. Some have only a mom, others have only a dad. Some have a stepparent, and others live with people who are not their parents at all (e.g., with other relatives or in foster homes).

When a divorce does happen, many act like it does not even bother them. It is supposed to be a normal part of life, so why should it upset me? And, even if it did, what would I do about it? So what. My parents got a divorce. Who cares if I feel ripped-off in the middle of the whole thing? *God cares.*

The Bible says that God hates divorce (Mal. 2:10–16). The reason He hates it is that He knows how much it hurts people like you and me. God never designed marriages to end. Jesus said, "Therefore what God has joined together, let man not separate" (Matt. 19:6). So, if your family has gone through a divorce and your heart and head are confused about it, don't feel like you are the one who has the problem. We will talk about how to get over the impact of a divorce in the next chapter (dealing with forgiveness).

How do you live day to day with your present situation? If your mom and dad are still single, or if one of them is seeing someone, what should you do? What if they get re-married? How should you deal with the stepparent? These are complex questions, and we must look to the Bible to find God's way of handling them.

Dealing with a Single-Parent Family

As a family separates after a divorce, many of the same dynamics take place as when a person dies. The sense of loss to the mother, if it is the father who left, is similar to a woman who has just become a widow. The emptiness she feels after part of her life has been torn away and her heart ripped out is only worsened by the fact that it was not an accident. She was devastated by the volitional choice of someone she loved.

The loss a young person feels is similar to what an orphan feels at the loss of his parents. It is like one or both of the parents are dead. They are bereaved, or in other words, deprived of the love and constant relationship with that person. It is as if they have had something taken away from them. They feel stripped, robbed of their security, and the permanence of the separation is like the permanence of death. America's teens are becoming orphans in their own homes.

How does God respond to a family without a father (or mother)? Hosea 14:3 says, ". . . in you the fatherless find compassion." He promises to help the fatherless (Ps. 10:14). He says He will be "A father to the fatherless, a defender of widows . . ." (Ps. 68:5). If you have gone through a divorce in your family, you have a very special place in the heart of

God. He looks at you the same as He does an orphan because you have gone through many of the same things. He promises to help you and stick with you through all the empty and lonely times.

If your parents are divorced and have remained single, don't feel like you need to take sides. You may have a tendency to favor the one you are living with because you hear his or her side of the story all the time. Just realize that it takes two to have problems. It is never just one who caused it. Both of your parents are imperfect, so don't idolize one over the other.

If one of your parents tries to put the other one down, you should ask that parent to stop immediately. You should not have to hear that about either of your parents from anyone. No matter what the problem is, you should not be put in the middle of it. They should not force you to choose between them just because they cannot get along with each other. It is wrong for them to ask or force you to choose sides or to ask you to get in the middle of their fights. Don't fall for the, "Just tell your father. . . ." Do not feel like you should have to take sides in their struggle. You should not even have to hear what their struggle is. You are not their referee! Ask them to get a counselor to do that! If they still have problems that they need or want to work out, let them know that you will NOT be the middle man. This will take a lot of self-control, because you will sometimes want to be that person. You still have the blood of both parents in you, and you should be proud of that and not ashamed.

The Bible says, "And my God will meet all your needs . . ." (Phil. 4:19). God knows exactly what you need, so ask Him for it. He will supply a father or mother for you if you need one. Many times He will give you a godly man or woman in your church family to fill that role in your life.

The word "parent" means "to nurture" like when you cultivate a garden. I have found that is what many teens want. They are looking for someone to love them and help them grow. That is what a real parent is. Someone who cares enough about you to help you grow up and mature. Just because they have the same blood you have does not mean they cultivate you and help you grow.

Look for people in your church who will help you grow. God will give them to you. He knows you need people like that more than you do. Seek out people you really respect at church and ask them to pour into your life. Obey them as if you were supposed to, because as they invest in your life like that, they really are playing the role of a parent. If you need a dad, God will give you someone from within your church who can play that role. The same is true if you need a mother. God will provide someone to nurture you and help you mature in your relationship with Him. Go to your pastor or youth pastor to ask him how to go about finding this person.

Stepfamily Harmony

Fifteen percent of children in the United States live with stepfamilies.[15] If you are living in one of those families, you can know that you are not alone. I realize that it sure does not make it any easier to cope with your situation, but at least you can know that there are others who understand what you are going through. It's not like, "Well, everything is going to be Okay now since there is a male and female figure in the home. Some parents think that getting a new spouse quickly will help to soothe the pain of the divorce. Their motive may be right, but the result does not usually accomplish what they wanted. Here are some things to watch for.

1. Spite–Driven Behavior

Many times your biological parents are still mad at each other when one or both remarries. They continue to think of ways to get even with the other person for the pain he or she caused. They may tell you things about your other parent while you are visiting them to try to get you mad at him or her. They may give you things to try to lure you away from the other parent and hurt the other. This becomes a game to them, and you are the pawn.

When I was seven years old my parents were divorced. Once, when I went to visit my dad, he held me up to kiss my stepmom while my mother was driving off. They may talk bad about your mom's or dad's new spouse just to keep you from liking him or her. The tragedy is that all this stuff just messes with your head even more. You have to learn to see through all these games. Just don't go along with them.

2. Guilt and a Divided Heart

So, you finally accept the fact that the parent you live with has gotten re-married. (Let's say your mom in this case, just to cut down on the confusion.) You decide you are going to try to get to know your new stepdad, and you find out that he is not that bad a person after all. In fact, you even like him. After a while, you start getting attached. Then you go and visit your father. You probably end up saying more than you should about your new relationship with your stepdad and you find some jealousy from your "real" dad. You start playing down how much you like your stepfather. Inside you start feeling guilty for even liking him at all! This new relationship is the thing your mom has been begging for, even praying for. However, now that you really like the guy, you feel as if you are betraying your dad. It seems like whatever you do, you cannot win.

Let me tell you: You have nothing to feel guilty about. If your biological parent is trying to make you feel bad about liking your new stepparent, it is his problem, not yours. You should never be put in that position in the first place! It is not even your fault you have a stepparent! Besides, just because you love your new stepparent does not mean you do not love your biological parent, or that you love him any less. Both your parents need to know that you love them no matter what kind of relationship you have with your stepparent.

It is easy to feel divided between your two families. You go to one house and you do not feel completely at home, and you go to the other home and you still do not feel like you are at home. So where is your real home anyway? It is a lonely feeling.

3. Stepparent Losing Out

Let's go back to your mom for a moment. Remember,

she was finally getting into a relationship after the divorce. After they are married you are determined to not get along with your new stepfather. You make him jump through every hoop you can think of; but you have decided ahead of time that no matter what he does, he will lose. There he is: working hard to pay for your food, clothes, and housing. He has loved not only your mom, but you and your brothers and sisters as well. He knew he was marrying into an entire family, and he is trying to be all that you need in a father, but you do not care.

In the midst of a disagreement you shout, "You're not my real dad anyway!" A statement like that cuts to the heart of someone doing all he knows to do to get inside your heart. You have to learn to make the best of your situation. You have to realize that your stepfather is a person too! How would Jesus treat him? Give him a break. Don't make him feel like the third foot. Be sensitive to your biological mother who really loves this guy and who really loves you. Your mom and dad are trying to do their best to pick up and go on with life. Give them a break, and try see your stepparents through the eyes of God.

As a teen, I moved in with my dad and stepmother. I was 15 and she was 26, and it was not my idea of a good time! We increasingly despised each other as the days went by. Finally, after I got turned on to the Lord, God began to draw our hearts together. I began to see her as an individual instead of a 26-year-old hag who wanted to boss me around. Later she gave her heart to the Lord and asked me to baptize her. We became the best of friends, sharing what God was doing in our lives and praying together regularly. It was an incredible change!

The Making of a New Family

One day, Jesus was talking to a crowd. Some people came to Him and said, " 'Your mother and brothers are standing outside, wanting to speak to you.' He replied to him, 'Who is my mother, and who are my brothers? . . . For whoever does the will of my Father in heaven is my brother and sister and mother' " (Matt. 12:47–50).

You cannot go through your life thinking you have only half a life because your family is not together anymore. Jesus had a whole different definition of family anyway. He said it was those who really loved His Father and did His will who were actually His family. You have to have more than just the same blood to be a close family. You have to have the same thing in your heart if you want to be really close. I know of Christian stepfamilies that are much closer than any natural family that is still together but does not have the Lord. It is more important to be in God's family together, than in a traditional one with your hearts all torn apart and going separate ways.

God can create a tighter bind than just a physical one. He is the one who pulls you together. He created the family to work the best with Him in the middle of it. Without that, you may have your biological parents together, but you will not be the kind of family that God meant for you to be. Only when each member of the family serves Him with all his heart can there be real oneness. Clearly Jesus set a new definition and standard for the family. It all revolves around His Father.

The bottom line is that if your parents try to get you in the middle of their fights, you have to be smart enough to not fall for it. If one parent lets you get away with murder and allows you to do sinful things (drink or smoke) without getting in trouble, *you have to be smarter than that.* Look for the person who is really nurturing you and helping you prepare for the future. THAT ONE is the person who is a parent in the truest sense of the word.

12

Forgiveness: Letting Go of the Past

As you can sense from these last few chapters, there are many complex issues in families today that are causing a lot of hurt. Too many arguments have been had and too many words have been exchanged that have scarred young people and their parents. We cannot pretend that these situations never happened. We cannot hope the bad feelings will just go away. We cannot just wish they were not there — wishing cannot make them suddenly disappear. We must learn to forgive.

Many things happen to us in life that just don't seem fair. It seems like every time we turn around, someone is ripping us off or stabbing us in the back. A lot of times it happens with someone we've been really close to, until all of a sudden he does something that really hurts us.

Family situations are a major source of real hurt. When the people we love most hurt us, it really stings our hearts. You may have been stabbed in the back, talked about, cut down, beaten, or even sexually abused. But don't think you are without hope. This chapter will tell you how you can be whole again and how you can restore lost relationships.

I want to encourage you that God's awesome power can

take away any pain no matter how deep it may be. The key to your recovery lies in the powerful principle called FORGIVENESS. Instead of just going through life and hurting, it's important for you to make a decision to deal with the hurt before you go any further. No relationship, fun, career, or activity can take away the pain of your past — only forgiveness can. When I was growing up, I had to deal with some forgiveness issues in my life as well. What I'm about to share with you, I know from experience will work.

My mom and I had a really tough time getting along as I grew up. I felt like she was constantly out to get me. It seemed like she always punished me worse than my brothers and sisters. She would say things to me that made me feel so low, I felt like flushing myself down the toilet. I grew up feeling so much hate towards my mom and I didn't have any idea how to get rid of it.

After I gave my life to the Lord, He began to deal with me about my mom. I had to change the way I felt towards her, and I didn't know how to do it. God spoke to my heart that I had to forgive my mom, but I had no idea how. What you are about to read is exactly the process God took me through to forgive her and believe me, it works!

When we are abused, the pain is often so deep it's hard to believe that it will ever go away. Unforgiveness doesn't affect the person who hurt you as much as it affects you when you hold onto it. It's like a weight on your shoulders that gets heavier every day you don't forgive. It's like a cancer in your heart that is infecting your whole body. It is almost like a dark cloud is following you around making you feel like you are the one to blame.

God has the power to heal your memories. When you forgive, the weight on your shoulders falls off. The cloud that's been following you leaves and the pain in your heart melts away. You won't forget every bad thing that ever happened to you. However, when you forgive, God takes away the sting and pain in those memories. It will no longer hurt to think of them.

Usually, when we get hurt, we get mad. It is hard for us to distinguish the difference between these two emotions, because we feel them both at the same time. The Bible says in Ephesians 4:26–27, " 'In your anger, do not sin': Do not let the sun go down while you are still angry, and do not give the devil a foothold." Sure, things are going to make you mad, but you have to know how to handle your anger when it comes. Many people have grown old and bitter at the world because they let anger and bitterness overtake them. God says do not even let one day go by while you are still mad. If you do, you give the devil a foothold in your life.

You can follow the Lord, go to church, and read your Bible every day. But if you get mad and stay mad, you invite the devil to put a stronghold on part of your life. It is like you are asking him to camp out right in your living room.

Ephesians 4:31–32 tells us how to deal with anger. "Get rid of all bitterness, rage and anger. . . . Be kind and compassionate to one another, forgiving each other, just as in Christ God forgave you." You get rid of anger by forgiving. It is the only way. No matter what you have been through, God has given you the power to forgive.

We all know that we should forgive. I'm going to give you some very practical steps on HOW to forgive.

Memorize Scripture

You have to be ready to do war if you really want to get rid of your pain. The way you fight this war is with God's Word. After years of dealing with this abuse, don't expect an instant answer with a quick little prayer. The devil has been cramming guilt and condemnation down your throat for years. Now it's time to cram some TRUTH in your heart concerning forgiveness. Study Scriptures like:

> For if you forgive men when they sin against you, your heavenly Father will also forgive you (Matt. 6:14).
> And when you stand praying, if you hold anything against anyone, forgive him, so that your

Father in heaven may forgive you your sins (Mark 11:25).

. . . Forgive, and you will be forgiven (Luke 6:37).

I can do everything through him who gives me strength (Phil. 4:13).

Write these and other forgiveness Scriptures down on index cards and take them with you everywhere. Meditate on them until you are saying them in your sleep. This is the first step toward your wholeness.

Make a Decision to Forgive

Forgiveness is not a feeling. You will never wake up one day and think, "Boy, I feel like forgiving today!" Our natural human tendency is to never forgive.

The definition of forgiveness is: giving up my right to hurt you back when you have hurt me first. The one who hurt you deserves to have you be very angry with him. No one is arguing with that. The whole idea is that we give up our right to strike back.

You cannot wait for God to tell you to forgive, He has already told you that you have to forgive (Matt. 6:14-15). It does not depend on the other person's repentant heart. You must forgive even if he never admits he did anything wrong. And it does not matter if you will never see him again. You can forgive him without seeing him. Forgiveness is between you and God.

Once you make the decision to forgive, the heaviness begins to lift off your life! A miracle happens in your heart!

Remember Stephen? As he was being stoned, he said, "Lord, do not hold this sin against them . . ." (Acts 7:60). Wow! Right in the middle of the stoning, he made a decision to forgive the very men that were killing him. You can decide right in the midst of people persecuting you to let go if it, with Jesus' power.

Stop right now. Think of all the people who have ever offended you (family or friends). Now, give all your anger and unforgiveness to the Lord. Ask Him to take it out of your heart. Take as long as you need. This book is not going to run off. You can get to the rest of the chapter when you finish, but stop now and deal with all the unforgiveness in your life.

Fight the Battle in Your Mind

Now you have made the decision and prayed the prayer, but the battle isn't over yet. You will not necessarily feel an overwhelming love for the person you forgave right away. Remember, forgiving him is not based on your feelings, but on a decision. You may have a tendency to think, "I don't feel any differently about the person or about my pain, so I guess I didn't really forgive him." WRONG!

If you made the decision, then you have forgiven. The devil will try to trick you into feeling condemned and confused about it. It is important to remember the date and time you prayed forgiveness, so you can remind the devil and remind yourself what you chose to do.

Fight the tendency to take up an offense and get mad again. Every time you have a thought about what happened, pull out those forgiveness Scripture cards and start quoting them.

The battle is in your mind. If you pull out your Scriptures every single time you are tempted to get angry again, there is NO question you will beat this thing. No one else can do it for you. Others can encourage you, but *you* must fight the battle.

As you continue to do this, you will begin to feel less and less pain. You'll find a growing love in your heart for the person who hurt you. You will discover the clouds are gone and you really feel free!

One last note: If you have been involved in sexual abuse, you should confide in your pastor or a qualified Christian counselor. It is imperative that you have someone HELP you work through these forgiveness issues, especially before you get married. It will keep you from many years of grief and marital struggles if you will take the time to do this now.

It may take weeks or months before you FEEL any different about the person who hurt you. Don't be discouraged. God's Word has the power to heal your broken heart. It NEVER fails! You just have to be committed to fighting your thoughts with His Word no matter how long it takes, because you know it's the right thing to do.

As you persist in your decision to forgive and in quoting God's Word, you will find the most incredible miracle happening in your heart. You will sense a freedom like you have never known before. The weight on your shoulders will fall off. The dark cloud that surrounds you will leave. God will perform a surgery that no surgeon can. He alone has the AWESOME POWER TO HEAL A BROKEN HEART.

Your healing can begin today, it all starts with your decision to forgive.

Section IV

The Hard Stuff

It seems like there are some issues that just cannot be categorized other than HARD STUFF. Today's teens are dealing with things that just a few years ago nobody even knew existed. Some issues are just a different version of an age–old problem.

If you are going to rise above the things that would try to bog you down, you are going to have to face these issues head on. It is time to start letting your Christian life affect every area of your life. No more tiptoeing around and trying not to hurt each other's feelings.

In the following chapters are a number of bold–faced decisions that you have to make in order to be a successful Christian through your teen years.

13

Teenage Bubonic Plague: Inferiority

There is an epidemic running rampant throughout this country. It infects the heart and home of every high school student and junior high student in this nation. From major cities to grassroots American towns, this fungus of the heart is taking its toll on teens.

This plague causes death just like the dreaded bubonic plague in Europe. This plague does not kill your body, it kills your dreams. It stifles your potential. It makes you feel worthless and paralyzed. It makes you feel like a loser before you have even had a chance to enter the game. Many teens feel unloved and unwanted as a result of this peril. It's called *inferiority*.

Peak years for major depression are between 15 and 19. Rates during those years are two to four times higher than in middle age, up to seven times higher than after age 65.[16] As a result of feeling so low, millions try alcohol or drugs. At least these things can take away the sting that comes from feeling like a nothing — at least they seem to, for a little while. So much effort has been spent trying to solve the drug problem. The way to solve the drug problem is to solve the esteem problem.

God wants to do great things through you as a teenager. There are awesome things that you have not even imagined that He has prepared for you to do. The problem is that too many teenagers end up not doing the things God has for them simply because they *don't think they can.*

Why Do We Think Like This?

This world constantly puts before us idols and heroes who are emulated by young people. As we see these different stars on TV we constantly compare ourselves with them.

As guys we are taught by society to look up to sports heroes. We see a "He Man" movie with Sylvester Stallone or Arnold Schwarzenegger, and immediately we think this is the definition of a real man. The more tough they are, the more lame we feel as a male.

We are led to believe that if we do not have hair on our chest and bench 250 pounds by the time we are 14 years old we are not really men. Something must be wrong with us. Society and friends make you feel strange if you are not sleeping with someone early in your teen years.

Jesus was the only real man who ever lived. If you want to be a real man, you have to look at HIS example. His passion was to be like His Father in heaven. It is not outer strength that makes a man, it is the inner strength of imitating the Almighty God!

Hollywood says you must be beautiful to be worth anything. All the model magazines make teenage girls feel like they *must* look like those models or they just will not survive their teen years. Let's think about it for a minute. The model they put on the front cover of a magazine has gone through a six– to eight–hour make–up session. All the stylists have worked over her hair, and her wardrobe has been extensively prepared. Then she will spend hours and hours at a photo shoot and have literally THOUSANDS of pictures taken of her. Then they will go back to develop them and choose one to put on the cover. Then they will go back to the lab and touch up the photo to make it look even better.

The picture then appears on the front of a magazine

where you see it and say in your heart, "I wish I looked like that!" The *model* wishes she looked like that!

It is a fake representation of reality. No one looks that good without a lot of work! Anyone could look like that if they had that many people working on them. Meanwhile, most teenage girls feel like they do not measure up because they don't look like the model on the cover.

Have you ever heard a girl say, "I'm fat!" You are looking at her thinking, "Girl, you are so skinny, you are going to blow away if you sneeze!" Maybe you have heard a beautiful girl say, "I am so ugly!" If you are a guy, you are thinking, "Baby, Baby, Baby, haven't you ever looked in the mirror?" It does not matter what you look like on the outside; if you feel worthless inside, you will think you are ugly.

More evidence of this plague is made known when people say, "How do I look?" or "Do you think I'm pretty?" all the time. Of course everyone likes to get a compliment, but some people are constantly fishing for them. They think that if they can get enough people to say they are okay, then they will feel okay about themselves. But it's not true. No matter how many compliments you get, they do not cure the problem.

It's kind of like having a car that you paint and make it look incredible on the outside. It looks incredible, but the engine runs like it's about to die, the upholstery looks ripped and ratty, and the transmission rattles. It does not matter how great it looks on the outside if it is a mess on the inside.

That is exactly how many teens are today. They concentrate so much on the outside with all the right clothes and makeup, but no matter what they do, they still feel like junk on the inside. It's time to fix up the inside of us so we can genuinely feel good about ourselves.

Sometimes it is our friends or family who make us feel like a nothing. The people you love can hurt you the worst with the words they say to you because you value their opinion so much. Just one comment like, "Boy, are you dumb!" from your dad is enough to make you feel like you need to go into a learning disability class.

Finally, there is the church. Many people are taught that God thinks we are worms. We are lead to believe that it is humble to think that we are nothing, insignificant specks of dust to God, and that we should grovel in the dirt and beg for mercy. After all, doesn't the Bible say, "Humble yourselves before the Lord, and he will stomp your head"? (James 4:10). NOT! It says ". . . He will lift you up!" That is the kind of God He is! He lifts you up because He thinks you are so valuable.

So, if you get all these messages from the media, your family, and friends telling you that you are not worth much, and then you hear it from a preacher, it just looks as if the evidence is conclusive. You think, *Well, if God thinks I'm a loser, too, then I must really be one!*

What Did Jesus Say about It?

Matthew 22:37–39 says, "Jesus replied: 'Love the Lord your God with all your heart and with all your soul and with all your mind.' This is the first and greatest commandment. And the second is like it: 'Love your neighbour as yourself.' "

Jesus is clear about what our priorities should be. He says that the first thing is that we should love God with all that we've got. The second command is just like it. In other words, it is so important that Jesus could not say the first one without mentioning the second one. He said you should "love your neighbour as yourself."

Many people think this means that you should love everyone else but not love yourself. They make a priority list that looks like this:

1. Love God.
2. Love others.
3. Love yourself.

If you look closer, that is not really what Jesus said. He said to love others AS you love yourself. That means that you must love others equally — as much as you love yourself. If you do not love yourself, you cannot love others. Oh, we try to, but it never really comes across as love. We put ourselves down and act like we are loving others because we are making others look good.

It sounds strange to say that we should "love ourselves." In fact, it sounds kind of prideful to say, "I love myself." Some would say, "Isn't that conceit and pride?" No, it is not. When we say, "Boy, that guy sure loves himself a lot," what we really mean is, "He is sure arrogant." Arrogance comes from low self-esteem. He, the arrogant one, feels so low about himself that he tries to make others believe that he is really something marvelous. He tries to push others around and make them feel weaker with his comments. He is the kind of person who really DOES NOT love himself. If he did, he would not feel he had to prove himself to anyone.

You can only love others as much as you love yourself. Anything else is just a vain servant mentality that makes you feel "good" the more you put yourself down.

Look at what Jesus told Peter about this. In Luke 5:8, Peter told Jesus, ". . . Go away from me, Lord; for I am a sinful man!" He had the same mentality that many people do today. "Go away from me Lord; I'm ugly, dirty, and worthless," is how a lot of us felt when we first discovered that Jesus was real. We have a tendency to push God away from us when we realize He is holy and we are not. But look at Jesus' response: ". . . Don't be afraid; from now on you will catch men" (Luke 5:10). He was saying to Peter, "I don't want you to push yourself away from Me, come towards Me. Do not be afraid!"

It was almost like a rebuke. "Peter! Get up off the ground! Stop that groveling! Quit crying and saying how worthless you are." Jesus said, "From now on you will be fishing for men!" He was telling Peter, "Peter, I see a great future for you. Now, stand up like a man! See yourself the way I see you. You are not a worm; you are going to do great things for God!"

Jesus asked the woman caught in adultery, "Woman, where are they [her accusers]? Has no-one condemned you?

. . . Then neither do I condemn you. . . . Go now and leave your life of sin" (John 8:10–11). He took a woman who had a lot of reasons to feel ashamed and worthless, and restored her dignity. If He would make her feel valuable, surely He would think highly of you.

It is not a sin to love yourself. It is holy. It is right. Jesus said it is the most important thing after loving God! It is a sin NOT to love yourself!

You would like to say, "Okay. So now I know I should love myself; how do I start?" I thought you'd never ask.

Stopping the Epidemic

There is only one cure. You have to believe the truth about yourself. God created you in His image. He does not make junk! The Bible says that He knit you together in your mother's womb and that you are fearfully and wonderfully made (Ps 139:13-14)! He got really excited the day you were born because you were another awesome example of His creation. The Bible says you can do everything through Christ who gives you strength (Phil. 4:13).

Now you have a choice to make. You can believe Hollywood or you can believe God. You can believe *Vogue* magazine or you can believe the Bible. It is your choice. The world runs you into the ground; God lifts you up. If you believe what the world says, you are calling God a liar. You are saying, "I don't care what you say, Lord, I still believe that I'm a loser." No wonder people feel lousy if they go around calling the Author of Truth a liar.

So, what do you do now? You start by repenting. That's right — repenting. "But," you say, "I'm already a Christian." That is great, but you still need to repent of your old way of thinking. You need to change your mind, to turn around. You need to ask God to forgive you for calling Him a liar. You need to commit to believing the truth and speaking the truth about yourself.

You need to say to yourself, "I don't care how I feel, I don't care what the world says. If God says I am valuable, then I am going to believe what He says about me instead of what I have always thought."

I love to tease people with mink coats. I always make a joke about it being dog hair. I will say something like, "What a beautiful dog hair coat you have. What was his name, anyway?" I am joking about something that is really valuable, and I am calling it worthless. Sometimes we do the same thing to the Lord, only it is not funny. We call ourselves worthless (like dog hair) when we have been washed in the mink coat of Jesus' blood.

An object is worth whatever you are willing pay for it. When I go overseas to different countries, I love to bargain for things. Now, if I leave a market after paying five dollars for a souvenir, to me that thing is worth five bucks. If I lost it, I would think I had lost five dollars' worth of stuff. When God decided to buy you back, He was thinking of what to pay for you. He could have paid with all the silver and gold in the world. He could have paid with all the diamonds and oil in the earth. But those were not enough. When He decided what to pay for you, He brought His own Son on the scene to shed His blood. That's how much you are worth to God, the blood of His only Son!

My Life

I grew up feeling pretty low. I felt like a complete failure and that I would never make anything out of my life. Even after I gave my life to the Lord when I was 16, I still felt like a loser. I was the guy everyone picked on in school, and everyone made fun of me. Finally, I got hold of one Scripture that changed my life. I had read it a million times before, but finally it came alive to me. "I can do everything through him who gives me strength" (Phil. 4:13). I read it again and again! I couldn't believe it God was telling me that HE believed in me! ME!! I, Ron Luce, could do ALL things through Christ! I thought, *Lord, in the midst of a world that has always told me I can't do anything with my life, here You are telling me I can do everything!*

Now I had a choice to make. I could believe what I always thought was true, or I could believe what God said about me. I thought, *God, if You said it about me, then I don't care what anyone else says; I'm going to believe what You say.* My life was completely changed that day. I began to look up every Scripture that I could find about who God thought I was, and I began to say them about myself. I thought, *If God can say it about me, then I can say it about myself!*

God wants to use you to change the world. Don't you dare let the inferiority the world tries to cram down your throat shut you down! Choose today to believe what God says about you! You will never be the same!

14

Music: The People behind the Tunes

Your relationship with Jesus should affect every area of your life. If He really came to live in your life, then His ways, His thoughts, and His ideas should begin affecting every area of your life, including music.

Who Invented It?

What is music? Why was it invented? Well, if you look back to Judges 5:3, it says, "...I will make music to the Lord. ..." As you read through the Bible, you see it talks about angels making music to the Lord in heaven, complete with trumpets blasting and harps playing. Music was invented to glorify God. It was invented as a way of expressing His majesty. Today we have music played by every culture and religion.

Let me clarify a couple of things: First of all, there is nothing wrong with music in itself. It was created to glorify God. The problem comes in the people who are expressing themselves in the music. What are they expressing?

Some people would say that it is a certain style of music that is wrong, such as rock and roll or heavy metal. The fact is that the style is not the issue. It is the CONTENT and the SPIRIT behind the music that is the issue.

Depending on what experiences the musicians have been through — if they have had good times or bad times, had experiences with drugs or alcohol, or been caught up in immorality — they will write a song based on their own perspective. When they do that, they are expressing themselves. Sometimes they are trying to prove a point; sometimes they are just expressing a thought or an idea that they have in their own head.

These musicians have taken the gifts that God gave them and are using them for themselves or for the world. Actually they are often using them for the devil, because many times they are presenting ideas that are not from the Lord. And if they are not from the Lord, then there is only one other source.

The problem with this whole issue is when we make a decision to listen to music whether or not anybody else likes it. Again, it is not the style of the music but rather the SPIRIT of the person who is writing the music.

If these people are still slaves to sin, rebellious against God or not wanting to have anything to do with Him, then they are writing music out of the old nature. When you listen to that music, you are letting it influence your mind. It is going in your ears, it is going into your head, and you begin to think about the words.

Remember, you have to be transformed by the renewing of your mind (Rom. 12:2). If you have your mind renewed by the Scripture and then go back to listening to that music, it simply tears down the Word of God that was planted in your mind.

Don't Just Do It

THE INFLUENCE OF DIFFERENT STYLES OF MUSIC — WHAT THEY ARE SAYING AND HOW

THEY ARE SAYING IT.

Music, especially in America and Europe, has become a subculture.

What I mean by this is that a certain kind of teen in any high school in America listens to a certain kind of music, whether it is pop or heavy metal or rap. In that style of music, a teen who listens to it may know all the groups that come out and all the things they sing about and have the latest CD's and videos. He begins to dress and even dance like the people on the videos.

When a group within a culture acts and speaks in a distinct way, that group becomes a subculture. It is a small group within a group. You may not even realize that you wear black all the time, do your hair a certain way, have a certain attitude, or say certain words from your music all the time.

The problem is, the subculture sucks you in and you do not even realize it. You are being trained to think the way they think, to sing the way they sing, to look the way they look, to act the way they act.

The Bible speaks very clearly about this in Exodus 23:2. It says, "Do not follow the crowd in doing wrong. . . ." Do not give in to peer pressure. Do not do what the world wants you to do just because the world wants you to do it.

Just look at what some of the different bands are singing about these days:

Style: Rock
Group: Areosmith

Lyrics: "Something wrong with the world today/the bulb is getting dim. . . .

These guys have made a comeback recently. This is a relatively easy–listening tune compared to the drugs and sex that they usually sing about. They are singing the blues of a world gone bad, but they have no answer for us. You can only cram that in your head for so long before you get depressed.

Style: Hip-Hop/Rap
Group: Salt–n–Pepa
   Lyrics: Children play, women produce, kids killing kids just for the juice, who gives a d — n about me?

   In addition to the usually sexually explicit music they sing, these gals are really depressed. Again, after you hear this about a million times you are going to start to think, "Who gives a d — n about me?"

Style: Grunge/Alternative
Group: Nirvana
   Lyrics: Stay away, God is gay — burn the flag, gotta stay, stay away.

You have probably heard about the lead singer from Nirvana, Kurt Cobain. He was so frustrated with life, and confused, that he shot himself in the head in April of 1994. This is just one blatant example of what cramming words like these into your head will do to you.

   Just because these guys are famous rappers or rock stars does not mean that what they say or do is right or that the way they dress is right. What ends up happening is that you let society and these groups tell you what to think, and you let them tell you what is cool and what is not cool. They are ripping you off, and you do not even realize it. You have to be strong and realize that their philosophies are working their way into the way you think and the way you live.

   You need to begin to measure the music you listen to by the words they are saying and compare them to the Word of God. Make your decision about whether to listen to certain kinds of music based on how it compares to God's Word. If it agrees with the Word then listen to it. If not, do not listen to it because you'll to be tricked into believing their ideas. As a result, your foundation in Christ will not be stable.

   Now is the time for you to get honest about getting rid of some of the music you listen to. If you have been wondering why you have been going up and down in your Christian walk, this could be the reason. Have the guts to do what is right. I want you to trash, throw away, get rid of, shove down the garbage disposal — whatever it takes — just LOSE ALL of your secular music.

This is not a casual suggestion — it is a matter of your spiritual survival! Do it right NOW! God will blow your face off with blessing you if you give your music life to Him.

MTV Influence

MTV has given free access to all kinds of bands that promote a lifestyle that mocks everything the Bible stands for.

MTV is in 231 million households worldwide (CNN is only in 100 million).[17] They proudly proclaim that they are a "cultural force. People don't watch it — they live it. MTV has affected the way a whole generation thinks, talks, and buys."

Yet they boast that they "listen to this generation and give them what they want." It looks more like they are manipulating a generation for their own gains.

Again, they boast, "The strongest appeal you can make is emotional. If you can make them forget their logic, you've got 'em. At MTV we don't shoot for the 14 year olds, we own them."

HOW DO YOU LIKE SOMEONE TELLING YOU HE OWNS YOU???

The problem is that 42 percent of Christian teens watch MTV compared to only 30 percent of non–Christian teens on any given week.[18]

What Are We Gonna Do about It?

When we are talking about the music we listen to, do we mean that instead of listening to rock and roll we should only listen to church songs or hymns and sing very spiritual songs?

NO, THAT IS NOT WHAT WE ARE SAYING!

It means that music is an expression of your heart, an

expression of an idea, an expression of something that you are thinking about or something that is going on inside of you. People write songs about the things that inspire them.

The Bible says that if you are going to sing a song, let it be a spiritual song — sing and make music in your heart to the Lord (Eph. 5:19).

Let the song talk about:

> how awesome God is,
> how cool God is,
> how great God is.

Don't waste your energy glorifying your ideas, an experience somebody else had, or another way of life. Let's sing songs that lift up the King of kings and the Lord of lords.

As we have already said, there is nothing wrong with the style of music itself. The important thing is: Who wrote the stuff you are pumping into your head? What was in his heart when he wrote it? That is what's going to get in your heart when you listen.

God has raised up many different music styles with people who have given their lives to Jesus. Try pumping this stuff into your brains instead and see what happens! (See Christian Music Alternatives in the back section.)

I sincerely believe that it is really important to not just blow your brains out with loud, wild (even Christian) stuff ALL THE TIME. No matter who you are or what style of music you like, it is imperative that you slow down and listen to some worship songs as well. Take the busyness and loudness out of your life long enough to really worship quietly in your heart. Who knows, you might actually hear HIS voice if you quiet everything else down!

Our Response to MTV

It is time for us as an ATF (Acquire the Fire) generation to stand up and let MTV know that they don't own us any more. You cannot just sit by and let them brainwash all of your friends and the entire teen culture (including you??).

We can DO something about it. If they are really listening to teens, then let them hear from some radical teenage fireballs.

The following page is a blank letter for you to copy. Write in what you think, tear it out, fold it, and mail it.

The People Behind the Music

The fact is, the people who are making the music are for the most part confused, on drugs, without hope, feeling like they have been ripped off. Many are flushing their future down the drain and don't even care.

What is even more important is what is going in the hearts of those writing today's most popular music. The Gangsta–rap and hip–hop tunes are laced with the hurt and hard times of young people being raised in the ghetto and having to fight for their lives. They rap about the injustices of the "system," and they portray someone who is really mad and hurt.

Alternative music, especially grunge, is sweeping the nation and the world right now. Many of these bands started small and never intended to get big. They write songs about how society has ripped them off. They talk about longing for the family that TV promised — like the Brady Bunch — but ending up in a single-parent home as a latchkey kid.

Millions of teens buy their albums, not because they provide happy answers to their problems, but because they can identify with the hurt they are singing about.

Band: Cranberries
    Lyrics: Crying helpless, I can't live for tomorrow, I will tear my heart out, I am by myself. . . .

Band: Pear Jam
    Lyrics: Daddy didn't pay attention to the fact that Mama didn't care

Band: Nirvana
    Lyrics: "I'm Dumb — or just happy" smells like Teen Spirit — Cubain "bellyaching about something I couldn't have, a solid form.

These guys sing about the pains of a family that has been torn apart, but they have no answers to the pain they feel. A whole generation of young people is following them because they feel the same way, but don't know what to do about it.

Kurt Cobain from Nirvana couldn't handle the pain anymore. Do you want to end up like him?

Maybe you can relate to that kind of pain. Jesus Christ has real answers to real pain. He is the only One who can take it away. He wants to do miracles today in the hearts of a brokenhearted generation.

It is not enough to identify with someone who is hurting, or with music that describes how you have been ripped apart. You need answers and hope. Jesus has both.

See chapter 12 about forgiveness if you are needing to deal with some of the pain from your past.

MTV
Attn: Viewer Services
1515 Broadway
New York, NY 10036

Date _____

Dear MTV,

My name is _____. I want to let you know that you DO NOT own me!

I will NOT watch your network. I am tired of all the sick videos (sex, violence, and drug abuse), as well as the other programming that portrays rebellion and lifestyles that have proven to wreck people's lives.

I am unplugging you from my home, and I am calling my cable company to ask that you be disconnected from our cable system.

When you begin to use your influence to shape my generation with some wholesome values, I will be happy to plug you back in.

_____

_____

_____

_____

Sincerely,

_____ age _____

15

Peer Pressure: Feeling Good about Not Fitting In

One of the strongest forces on teenagers today is the pressure they feel from others their age. This pressure will manipulate, change, and even completely rearrange a person's lifestyle. The power of this pressure causes teens to fix their hair differently, wear different clothes, and change the way they spend their free time. It even begins to dictate the things young people do when their parents are not around — things that could drastically damage their lives!

Countless teens have begun smoking, drinking, shooting up, snorting up, or somehow getting drugs into their system, just because of the pressure they have felt from others their age. Too many have lost their dreams, their hopes, their goals, their future, and even their lives by doing something that a so-called "friend" put pressure on them to do.

Maybe you remember the story about Robert. He wanted to join a gang. He was 11 years old and grew up in the Chicago area. His so-called "friends" in the gang said that he needed to kill someone if he wanted to join. So Robert took a gun and killed a 14-year-old girl.

The police discovered who had done it and that the gang "friends" had put him up to it. The gang members got scared and took Robert out and shot him in the head. His life was destroyed because of so-called "friends."

Why? Why? Why?

One of the biggest reasons that young people give into the pressure is their desire for acceptance from others their age. Everyone wants to be liked by others. The struggle is: What will you do to get them to like you? How low will you stoop to please them? If you have to stoop so low that you go against what you believe, is getting their approval worth more than how low you feel when you compromise your standards?

So many teens feel so insecure that they will do whatever they have to do in order to get their peers to accept them. They want so badly for others to like them that they forget all about what they said they would never do. They equate their self–worth with how many people like them. They think that if the popular people at school do not think they are worth liking, then they must not be worth much.

THE CORE PROBLEM OF PEER PRESSURE IS THAT TEENS ARE GETTING THEIR SELF-WORTH FROM THEIR PEERS RATHER THAN FROM GOD. As we discussed in chapter 13, if you know what God thinks of you, it won't matter what others say about you. You have to believe God's opinion more than you believe the opinions of other teens around you. You have to choose to value His thoughts about you more than you value their thoughts.

How to Stand Against Peer Pressure

1. Know You Are Right

The story of Shadrach, Meshach, and Abednego gives us a perfect plan of action to follow when we are faced with peer pressure. If you remember Daniel 3, King Nebuchadnezzar made a huge statue of himself and commanded everyone to bow down and worship it whenever they heard the music. Talk about peer pressure, this was the whole country doing the same thing, not just a group of popular people at school.

Just imagine Shadrach and his buddies thinking about this new law. They were Jews. Jews were only supposed to worship God, never some idol made out of metal. They knew that it was not right to worship something that was made from men's hands. They had made a commitment to God: to serve and honor Him only. They knew it was the right thing to do even if EVERY SINGLE PERSON in the country worshipped the idol.

We start wondering if what we are doing is right, especially when we see almost everyone else doing the opposite. You have to have confidence that living for God is the right thing to do. You do not want to be arrogant, just confident. Living a radically sold–out life, passionately going after Jesus is the BEST thing you can do with your life. Living totally pure and holy before God is the only thing that matters.

After all, just think about it. You are going to heaven, they are not. You are the one who has been forgiven, they have not. You are the one God is pleased with, they are not. You are on the right side, they are not! You are right! You did what pleases God, you gave your life to HIM! They are wrong. Just because there are a lot of them does not mean they are correct. So do not be intimidated by a bunch of wrong people!

2. *Make a Decision Beforehand*

Shadrach and his friends knew they were going to be asked to bow before the idol. They were not pretending that the king would never play the music. They were realistic about it. They knew they were going to have to make a choice about it.

Sometimes we walk around thinking that we won't really face the temptations that everyone else faces. We act like the pressure that others put on us is not really real. We do not realize that we are walking right into a temptation extravaganza every time we go to school.

Shadrach made a decision beforehand — he knew exactly what he and his friends would do when the music played. They did not wait until the heat of the moment and just make something up when the music played. They had it planned out. They knew exactly what to say, exactly what to do. Then when they got into the situation, they just did what they had planned.

This is a great idea for you. Plan out in advance exactly how to respond to your peers. Think about what you will say when someone invites you to a party to drink. Know exactly what to say when someone teases you about not being sexually involved before you are married. Rehearse in your mind everyone laughing at you because of your radical stand for God and then exactly what you will say (or not say) in response to them.

God will give you some one-liners that will pierce their heart if you really pray about it. Jesus had some of the greatest one-liners in the world! In fact, it becomes a lot more fun to be different and not fit in just to see how your one-liners will affect them each time!

Shadrach's instant response was to do the right thing when faced with temptation, because he and his friends had planned it in advance. Your response should be instant as well if you plan in advance to do what is right.

3. Willing to Do Whatever It Takes

Shadrach, Meshach, and Abednego knew what the penalty was for not worshipping the king's statue. Everyone knew. The king had announced that everyone who did not bow would immediately be thrown into a blazing furnace (Dan. 3:6).

There would be no second chance. They knew what to expect if they did not bow, but they stood firm anyway. The king brought them in and gave them a second chance, but they responded by saying one of the most courageous, convincing lines ever said by young people (remember, they were young like you).

> If we are thrown into the blazing furnace, the
> God we serve is able to save us from it, and he will
> rescue us from your hand, O king. But even if he
> does not, we want you to know, O king, that we will
> not serve your gods or worship the image of gold
> you have set up (Dan. 3:17-18).

They were willing to die for what was right. Are you?
Even if it costs you everything, will you go for it? It is only
when you make the decision to go for it no matter what it
costs you, that you really experience the freedom of living
for Jesus. That is exactly what He asked for when you gave
Him your life: everything.

You have to realize you are in a war. So get ready to
fight! Most of the people in this world are on the losing side,
and they do not even know it. When you are in a war, you
have to do whatever it takes to win.

You have to have the determination that no matter what
your peers do to you, you will not back down. After all, what
is the worst they could do to you? Kill you? I think not. What
are they going to do, call you a name? Oh, no! Those big
mean people! Do you think they will spit on you? So what.
Will that kill you? If you know that God approves of you, it
does not really matter if some punk–faced, two–bit, heathen
teenager approves of you or not!

4. Surround Yourself With Radical Friends

If you noticed, Shadrach was not alone in his decision
to stand up for what he believed. He had his homeboys —
Meshach and Abednego — on his right and left. They were
a threesome. They decided to go for it together! They had
made a commitment to God and they were helping each
other stand up for the commitment they had made.

You cannot try to live this Christian life by yourself.
You cannot be successful if your best friends are not saved
or if they are halfhearted Christians. If the only time you see
a Christian teenager is at youth group, then you have the

wrong group of friends at school. If you are stuck right in the middle of intense peer pressure at school every single day, all by yourself, it is going to be easy to fall for the temptation to follow the crowd.

If Shadrach had been hanging out with a group of people who were bowing down to the statue, it would have been harder for him to stand for what was right. If Meshach and Abednego bowed to the idol, Shadrach might also have fallen to his knees.

The same is true for you. If you are hanging around those who are involved in stupid, sinful stuff all they time, you will get sucked into it, too. Find some fired–up friends to hang out with! See chapter 17 for more details.

5. *Create Righteous Peer Pressure*

Because Shadrach and his pals kept their commitment, God blew away their enemies. You probably remember that when they got thrown into the furnace, they did not get burned up. In fact, they had a visitor.

The king looked in and said, ". . . Look! I see four men walking around in the fire . . . and the fourth looks like a son of the gods" (Dan. 3:25). Jesus had come to hang out with them in the fire. He will come and hang out with you every time you are persecuted, too!

The king said, "Come out!" Nebuchadnezzar wanted to know what kind of men these guys were. What was it about them that made them not bow when everyone else did. And why weren't they burning when they were thrown in the fire. And just who was this fourth guy anyway? After spending time talking with these three amazing young guys, he made a law that everyone must worship the God of Shadrach, Meshach, and Abednego! He demanded that no one say anything against their God! How is that for righteous peer pressure? Then He promoted them on His staff!

We, as Christians, need to start exerting godly, righteous peer pressure. As we stand up for God, He will vindicate us in front of our friends. In other words, HE will start proving that He is right, and that we are right for following Him. When they start seeing God's blessing on your life — how you have peace and confidence no matter what — they will want what you have. When they see that you stand for what you believe no matter what it costs you, they will know that you have something that is real.

After all, this is not just a matter of "What I believe is better than what you believe." You believe the truth — the only way to heaven. You don't just believe words written thousands of years ago; you have a relationship with a living God. Since you have given your life to Jesus, He is living inside you right now. He has changed you from the inside out! He is not a *little* bit better; He is the *only* thing that is worth giving your life for.

We ought to have the attitude: "What? You are NOT saved? You are blowing it, dude! You aren't happenin'! You mean you aren't going to heaven? You are getting ripped off and don't even know it!"

It is time for every young person who calls himself a Christian to stand up like Shadrach and be counted. Let us show this world that we are more serious about our walk with God than they are about the petty things they believe.

It feels great to be on the right team. All the angels, the awesome forefathers (like Abraham and others), and the Father, Son, and Holy Spirit are on your side. If you have their approval, who else's approval do you really need anyway?

16

The Baal of the '90s: Teen Idols

Our society is filled with a number of different ways to spend your time. In fact there are so many things that compete for your time that companies spend millions of dollars on advertising for just a few seconds of your time. They know that if they can get a few seconds, it could lead to your spending a lot more time, and eventually your money, with them.

So many different things pull on us for our attention. Different products in our society are marketed and geared to look bigger than life and to take you in. As you begin to spend your time on a particular activity, it begins to mesmerize you and even control you. It controls you in the sense that you start to plan your day around it and make everything else in your life fit in around it.

This is called an idol. The dictionary defines an idol as: An image of a god used as an instrument of worship, any object of excessive devotion or admiration.

We usually think of worship in terms of church or singing, but there are a lot of ways to worship something. Worship is defined as reverence or devotion for a deity, extreme devotion or intense love or admiration of any kind, to love greatly, adore and honor highly.

In our society there are so many things that get this kind of attention from us. The problem is that the only thing that deserves this kind of love and devotion is God, and these things can take our attention away from Him.

Baal in Scripture

Baal was a god worshipped by the Canaanites in the Old Testament. They believed he would bring them the right weather for good crops. The Jews were supposed to get rid of all the gods like this when they moved in and took over the land, but they failed to do so.

The people worshipped the idol of Baal in a number of different ways. They made sacrifices to statues of him, gave money to him as a sacrifice, and sometimes offered human sacrifices. The priests of Baal danced with frantic shouts and cut themselves with knives to excite the attention and compassion of the god. Their entire lives revolved around this idol, who was not alive.

When the Jews did not get rid of all of the Baal statues when they came into the land, some of them began to worship the idols as well. These were the people who were supposed to be worshipping the living God, and now they were worshipping an idol carved out of a rock.

Statues of Baal were scattered all throughout Israel so that virtually any Jew who wanted to worship this false god had plenty of opportunities to do so. At any time they could get sucked into spending their time on, and letting their life revolve around, something that was a lie.

Today's Baals

Today we have lots of idols scattered throughout our land like so many Baals. We have inanimate objects that steal our time and devotion.

Things

Walkmans: Teens listen to so much music, and many

constantly keep their earphones plugged into something, Their time revolves around who they are going to listen to next. They are sure to have withdrawals if you take away their headphones.

TV/VCR: Many hours are spent watching TV each year, even more than in a classroom! Many Americans schedule their lives around what is on the tube. They faithfully watch a particular show as if the program counted on them. Many take pride in the fact that they "always watch my program!" They would never let anything interrupt them!

Video–games: This craze has taken over the hearts and minds of young people everywhere. If it is not the high–tech Sega and Nintendo in the home, then it is the Game Boys while riding in cars or on planes. Millions of teens every year spend hour upon hour in a daze in front of a screen. These young people know every game available and exactly when new updates are coming out.

Computers: Teens and adults alike are being pulled onto the information superhighway. So much is constantly becoming available for computers that it becomes a religion for some just to keep up with it. It may start with interest in computer games and then graduate to serious study, use, and adoration of the machine.

Cars: This becomes the goal and central pivotal point of a teen's entire existence. They see their life as "Pre–car" or "Post–car." All their savings, time, and attention is put toward that first set of wheels. Then, once they get it, they pour all their money into maintaining it. They spend all their time washing it. They spend all their time thinking about it, or what they are going to do in it, or where they are going to go with it.

Money: Many people in America and around the world are preoccupied with it. They will do anything for it. Poor people and rich alike are controlled by it. The poor are controlled because they think about it so much and wish they had it and dream about what they would do with it. The rich are consumed by worry that they might lose it, or that someone is going to rip them off.

Careers: Many people let their life revolve around their present career or around pursuing the one they wish they had. They begin to worship the idea of "climbing the corporate ladder" and the prestige and power that would give them. They begin to pour all their energy into getting to the top. They will run over anybody, and do whatever it takes, right or wrong, to get there.

People

Music Stars: So many of the musicians today are idolized like gods. They are presented in concert with all the lights, sound, and video screens to make them seem bigger than life. There seems to be so much power in the arena when you walk in, that it is hard to realize that it might be just a few scrawny guys beating on some instruments and getting rich off the fantasy they have created about themselves. People buy CDs, videos, shirts, and posters, and plan their life around the next music release. They scream and go into a frenzy when these bands appear on stage. (Sound like anyone I mentioned earlier?)

Even in Christian music, the idolization has become way overblown. Yes, the Christian artists may be well-known, and they may play good music, but this is no reason to worship them. They are human beings, saved by grace and trying to minister to us. Just because they are saved does not mean we have the right to idolize them the way the world does to its stars. When we put these artists on such high pedestals, we put extreme, undue, ungodly pressure on them to somehow live up to the world's ideas of a music idol. It is dangerous for you and for the artist, and it is wrong.

Movie stars: We see them on the silver screen and somehow they look invincible. The character they are playing may be invincible, but the character is not real. People begin to live a fairy tale of wanting to be like a particular star or a character they have seen portrayed in a movie. They cannot wait until the next movie comes out where their favorite star is featured. In some cases, it becomes like a cult following.

Sports personalities: Many athletes seem bigger than life. Their incredible talents make them seem legendary. You see them in all kinds of magazines, on cereal boxes, and on TV programs. From the time you are young, people tell you that you should want to be like them. Countless hours every week are devoted to watching a particular team or sport around the tube. Untold lists of statistics are memorized to keep up with a sport or particular players. After all, anybody who makes that much money must be pretty extraordinary, right??

If you happen to be an athlete you could get caught up in the idolization of the sport or your own ability. You work very hard day after day, focusing only on what you could be one day. Your whole life begins to revolve around your sport. You have extreme devotion to it and cannot wait to do it again. It became an idol.

Boyfriends and girlfriends: Many young people have made an idol of the one with whom they are romantically involved (or the one with whom they wish they had a romantic involvement). They think about him all the time and long to be with him. They "worship the ground he walks on." They will do whatever they have to do to please the person, even of it violates their own principles. They are mesmerized by this person and cannot dare to think about what life would be like without him. He is a human idol.

What am I trying to say? Obviously there are some people we are going to like more than others and some interests we are going to appreciate more than others. We have to be careful of the place we give these things get in our hearts. Are we using them, or are they using us? Are we taking advantage of them, or are they taking advantage of us? Do we own them, or do they own us?

Have we let that person or thing become the central figure around which our whole life revolves? If so, it is probably an idol. Is it the center of your heart? If it is, it is probably an idol. Jesus wants to be the only thing in the center of your heart!

Do you revere, honor, and show extreme devotion to anything as much as you do to Jesus? If you do, it is probably an idol. These are expressions of worship. Maybe you never intended to, but you might be worshipping one of these convenient idols of the '90s.

This is why Jesus said the most important commandment is to ". . . Love the Lord your God with all your heart and with all your soul and with all your mind" (Matt. 22:37). God has to be number one and nothing should be a close second.

If you have one of these examples as a supreme figure in your life taking a lot of your time and thought, it is an idol, and you need to get rid of it now. Just repent. Ask God to forgive you, and start spending at least some of the time you would have spent thinking about that idol reading the Word instead.

You must guard your heart. There are idols scattered all through the land trying to steal attention and devotion from your heart. God the Father is the only One worthy of ALL the devotion that can come from your heart.

17

Friend till the End: In-Your-Face Friendships

What is a friend? According to the dictionary, a friend is "one attached to another by affection or esteem." A friend is someone you enjoy so much that you want to be with him whenever you can. A friend is someone to whom you are committed.

One of the problems that teens have with developing deep friendships is that they spend so much of their time with *things* that it severely limits their ability to interact with people. There are so many high–tech toys, walkmans, stereos, cars, TVs, and just *stuff*. The more time you spend with these things, the less time there is to spend with other people. The problem is that many teens spend more time with stuff than they do with people.

My wife, Katie, and I have two little girls. We teach them that they should only love something that can love them back. This means that we can only love people and not things. These days, the word LOVE is thrown around so much that it is hard to tell what we really love. So now my girls are the "Love Police" at home. Any time we accidentally say, "I just love this food," they are quick to shout, "No, you don't! You LIKE the food!" Of course, they are right.

Consequences of Bad Friendships

Bad friendships can lead you away from God, confuse you, and make you feel lonely. They can leave you feeling ripped off, stabbed in the back, get you into trouble and break your trust. One bad friendship can wreck your entire future (1 Cor. 15:33). This means we need to really think about who we choose to hang out with. We do not just accidentally find friends who will help us grow in God, we have to actively seek them out.

A lot of times after someone makes a commitment to live for God, he goes back and hangs out with his same old friends. The problem is that his old friends drown out what God is trying to do in his life. They put peer pressure on him to do the things he used to do and to see his Christianity as a passing religious experience. They think it is just a phase that everyone goes through at some time in his life.

Other young people who recommit their life to live radically for God get sucked back in with their halfhearted Christian friends in their youth group. These are the teens who sit in the back and make fun of everyone who really wants to seek God. They wonder why they keep going up and down in their walk with God, yet they keep hanging out with those who are lukewarm and mock those who are serious about their walk with God.

It is incredibly important to make new radical friendships once you have completely committed your life to Jesus. You may need to cut off friendships with people from your past life. You might need to end your friendships, or at least quit hanging around with those who are not saved. It also means you may have to cut off those who are only halfhearted in their walk with God. The old friends probably will not understand why you are doing it, but God will.

Levels of Friendships

ACQUAINTANCES — These are people we know, and we may even refer to them as friends. You may have gone to the same classes with them for years, but the fact is, you really know nothing more about them than their name. These people usually have a lot of peer pressure influence on us even though we actually are not very close to them. This is the lowest form of friendship.

PSEUDO–CLOSE FRIENDSHIPS — Another name for this kind of friend is "social friends." This is where the majority of teens are in their friendships. They say they are friends but they do not really know each other. These are people that you might hang out with at school, play sports with, or even go to youth group with. It is kind of a fake closeness. It happens a lot with junior high students as they proudly announce, "This is my best friend," and two days later, "I hate him!"

This kind of friendship is often found in youth groups. The teens go to camp together, have cookouts together, and meet in the same room for youth group meetings every Wednesday night for years. They sing, "Kum Ba Yah," and, "Friends are Friends Forever," and every one feels goose bumps together. They cry together at the altar every chance they get. The truth is that they hardly know each other. It is a false sense of closeness.

Gangs all over North America have these kinds of friendships. They think they are close because they dress the same way and hang out together. They feel secure because they have others who are looking for friendships, but have they really found close friends?

CLOSE FRIENDS — These are people you have really taken some time to get to know. There may be only a few people in your life you would classify as "close friends." Being a friend like this requires that you let down your guard and let someone know you for who you really are. This is kind of scary for some people because they hide behind a mask most of the time. So many teens in youth groups fail to develop close friends even within their youth group because they are afraid to be gut–level honest with others in their group.

Gang members sometimes develop these kinds of friendships because they can relate to their down–and–out experiences. They take creeds to "be there for each other" if they ever need each other. The problem is that human nature causes a person to look out for number one. So they may not find out until it is too late if their friend will really stick with them or not.

Christians have the best possibility for developing close friends since their lives are centered in Jesus Christ.

IN-THIS-TILL-THE-END FRIEND — This is the highest form of friendship known to mankind. This is the kind of relationship that ends up changing the world. Paul and Silas had it. Moses and Aaron had it. Elijah and Elisha had it. Jonathan and David had it.

Jonathan and David — How They Did It

Let's look at Jonathan and David's friendship to see what it was like and how it got that way.

1. What pulled them together.

First, let's look at Jonathan. He was the kind of guy who had a lot of guts and wanted to do something for God. First Samuel 14 tells the story of how the Israelites were surrounded by the Philistines out in the middle of nowhere. Jonathan had an itch. He saw all the other soldiers (about 300 of them) scared and confused, and he did not want to be one of them. He took his armor bearer and said, "Let's go and look at those guys and just see what happens, maybe God will act on our behalf."

He had an idea: Just maybe God will do something great. Maybe God will blow them off the face of the earth. Jonathan had courage to live on the edge for God, even if it meant risking his life for Him.

However, Jonathan had a problem. He was hanging out with an army who was a bunch of yellow–belly, chicken–liver, thumb–sucking babies! They were weasels! How could he have a real friendship with guys like that? Who in the world could be his friend?

Then one day, he came across another battlefield. It was once again the Israelites and the Philistines, but this time the Philistines had a giant fighting on their side. All of a sudden Jonathan saw a 17–year–old guy with a rock in his slingshot ready to take on the giant. As you know, David hit Goliath in the head and killed him (1 Sam. 17). But that was not good enough. Just like a normal teenager, David wanted to do something to really make the point. So he went and cut off Goliath's head and brought it to the king.

I can just imagine how excited Jonathan was to find someone else who had the guts to stand up for the Lord. Finally, he found someone who could relate to his desire to do something wild for God. I can feel the excitement he felt when he grabbed David and hugged him and probably said something like, "I finally found my friend!" First Samuel 18:1 says they became "one in spirit."

THE FIRST INGREDIENT FOR A FRIENDSHIP LIKE JONATHAN AND DAVID HAD IS A PASSION TO LIVE ON THE EDGE FOR GOD.

2. They loved each other as much as they loved themselves.

First Samuel 18:1 says they loved each other like this. They looked out for each other's good before their own. In 1 Samuel 20:8, David referred to himself as Jonathan's servant. In fact, at the end of 1 Samuel 20, we see a remarkable example of this attitude.

Here King Saul (Jonathan's dad) is telling Jonathan that as long as David is alive Jonathan will never get to be the king (because people liked David so much). He wanted Jonathan to bring David to him so he could kill him. Jonathan refused. He would NOT betray his friend even if it meant he would not be the next king. This is true SELF-LESSNESS!

This is why Christians have the best possibilities of being this kind of friend. You do not have to look out for number one any more, God looks out for you. You can really rejoice when your friend gets blessed or gets a promotion. You never get jealous, because you want his best. Jesus said, "Greater love has no-one than this, that he lay down his life for his friends" (John 15:13).

Recently I learned of a friend of mine who just had a great blessing happen to him. His name is Kirk Pankratz and he is the director of another youth ministry, called Youth America. I found out that he had been given the money to buy an old airport and that he was going to convert it into a compound for his summer camp. I was so excited for him. I have been asking God for years for a compound for Teen Mania and it would have been easy to get jealous of him. Instead, I had true joy in my heart that he was getting to see his dream come true before his eyes.

THE SECOND INGREDIENT: SERVING EACH OTHER AND WANTING EACH OTHER'S BEST.

3. They made a covenant together.

First Samuel 18:3–4 describes the kind of commitment they made: "And Jonathan made a covenant with David because he loved him as himself. Jonathan took off the robe he was wearing and gave it to David, along with his tunic, and even his sword, his bow and his belt."

They made a promise to stick with each other until the end. They were out to help each other succeed.

This kind of friendship is called ACCOUNTABILITY FRIENDSHIP. These kinds of friends make a commitment to help each other grow in the Lord. It is a commitment to push each other to get closer to God. It is giving your friend permission to GET IN YOUR FACE!

When you make this kind of commitment, you tell your friend, "I'm going to help you become that radical fireball for God that you told me you wanted to be." It means that you say, "I love you too much to let you backslide, sin, compromise, or mess up your life."

It is hard to backslide if someone cares about you and asks you every day, "How was your quiet time with God today?" (See chapter 4.)

In this level of friendship, you share your greatest fears and really pray for each other. You are determined to go after God with all you've got and to change the world together.

THE THIRD INGREDIENT: A COMMITMENT TO AN ACCOUNTABILITY FRIENDSHIP.

It is time for you to get a friendship like this. You cannot try to live the Christian life with only a bunch of shallow friendships around you (especially if some of these friends are not even Christians). You are going to have to cut off close friendships with those who do not know Jesus and with those who are halfhearted for God. At the very least, you can no longer have these people as your closest friends.

It is time to let someone get in your face. It is time to get an ACCOUNTABILITY FRIENDSHIP.

Here are some things you can commit to do with your accountability friend:

1. Pray for each other. Really listen to what each other is going through and pray for each other.

2. Do the same Bible study together like *56 Days Ablaze* . . . commit to finish it.

3. Ask each other every day, "How was your quiet time today?"

4. Plan to change the world together this year (i.e., plan to go on a mission trip together or invade your school together this year).

5. Plan to stick with each other for at least one year and serve each other with a selfless attitude.

Find your IN–IT–TILL–THE–END FRIEND TODAY! That person will help you grow in the Lord maybe more than anything else in your life. That is a true friend.

I commit to be a
"COMMITTED, COURAGEOUS, I'M-IN-THIS-TILL-THE-END FRIEND"

with you and to keep all
five of the below
commitments with you.

_____

Signed (your name)

_____

Signed (friend's name)

1. Pray for each other. (Really listen to what the other is going through and pray for each other.)
2. Do the same Bible study together, like *56 Days Ablaze* . . . commit to finish it.
3. Ask each other every day "How was your Quiet Time today?"
4. Plan to change the world together this year (i.e., plant to go on a mission trip together or invade your school together this year).
5. Plan to stick with each other for at least one year and serve each other with a selfless attitude.

Section V

Doing Something That Counts

"Something that matters." "Something to sink your teeth into." "Something that will make a difference." These are the things I hear teens all over America asking for. It is not enough to just have fun during your teen years. It is not enough to have all the high–tech toys you could possibly imagine. There must be something more.

There is.

God has an incredible plan for you to be involved in changing the world. Indiana Jones eat your heart out! God has a REAL mission for us. It will demand your all. It will push you out of your comfort zone. It will cost you all you have, including the plans you have made for your own life.

It will give you the greatest rewards. It will be the most adventure you could possibly imagine. It will be more fun than a human should be allowed to have on earth.

It is God's big plan for you. These last few chapters will keep you from EVER having just a boring Christian life again, if you just do what is laid out for you!

18

Finding Your Purpose in the Cause

Many teenagers today are looking for something to really pour their lives into. They see all the things that their parents have poured their guts out for and are not easily drawn to do the same thing. Today's young people see that their parents have sold their soul for the American dream. They work for it. They live for it. They cannot wait for the second car, vacation home, and the boat. They work hard for these things, many times at the expense of their family. A lot of teenagers have all the toys they could possibly want, yet they feel far away from their parents. Their family has fallen apart. As a result, there are a lot of young people who don't really care about getting all the "stuff" in life. They do not want to pour their lives into the shallowness of just having things. They want to find out why they are really here.

They want a purpose that they can really sink their teeth into. Something they can give their all for. Something that will demand their all, yet when they are done they will know it was worth it. Purpose gives you a reason to get out of bed every morning. It is hard to have a sense of purpose if you are going to a mundane job every day just trying to inch your way up the ladder and looking out for "Numero Uno."

This is what the whole "Generation X" thing is about: young people trying to find something that will fulfill them. They want to find what they were born to do.

God created you to do something great for His kingdom! This is real purpose! When you get hold of His purpose for your life, you find the zest of life.

Many people try to find their purpose by getting involved in a cause. They think that if they get into something that is helping others or protesting something that is bad, then their existence will be justified.

The fact is, God already has a cause for you. Actually, it is THE CAUSE. When you find your purpose in THE CAUSE, you really discover what you were born to do. And there in nothing like getting involved in the biggest CAUSE in the history of mankind!

As a teenager, I wanted to do something big for God. I just wanted to minister somehow in a meaningful way to people who really needed it. I thought I might be a youth pastor or a traveling minister, but nothing really seemed to fit. Then, I discovered THE CAUSE!

It was like my eyes were opened and I could finally see the BIG PICTURE of what God was really trying to do in the world. It was so thrilling to think that I could be involved in the most important thing in the history of mankind: Not talking about it, but actually reaching the world!

There is a place for everyone in His Cause, and I hope you begin to discover yours by the end of this chapter.

What Is a Cause?

A cause is a response to a problem or a predicament. It demands that something be done. The problem gives you a big reason (a cause) to respond. It gives you a reason to do something radical. The problem may demand you do more than you ever thought you could do in order to answer the problem. It's like a good Clint Eastwood movie where he says, "Go ahead, make my day!" Just give me a reason to do something ballistic!

In 1 Samuel 17, David found Israel in a predicament.

Goliath had come out to challenge the army of Israel and no one would do anything about it. David saw the situation and cried out in verse 29, "Is there not a cause?" (KJV). He was saying, "Isn't anybody going to do something about this? Don't we have a response to this bully?" The implied answer is, "Of course we do!" David responded and killed Goliath.

God made us with the desire to pour all of our guts into something. Every human being has something in him that says, "I want to do something significant, something that matters in life, something important." That is why the Bible says, "Whatever you do, work at it with all your heart . . ." (Col. 3:23).

Examples of a Cause

America is plagued with all kinds of petty causes. Remember, a cause is a response to a problem. So, for example, a teen may have a problem in that he wants more clothes. His response to that problem is to complain to his parents or to work hard to get some new ones. For a while, this might be his cause. Or, for example; let's say the problem is that someone wants a boyfriend or girlfriend. (Of course, I'm not talking about you since you have already read chapter 7.) So the average teen's response to that problem is to go crazy trying to get one. It becomes a cause, a whole reason to live. Many will do WHATEVER it takes to get one.

Maybe you have heard of a situation where a teacher is unfairly fired from her job. This is a problem that students rally around and protest. Some have even gone on strike and walked out of classes because of it. Their response is, "It is not fair!" Thus, they make a cause out of it.

The world is full of so many different causes. People are trying to find purpose by pouring their lives into something. They go from cause to cause, never staying with any one cause for very long, and never finding satisfaction or fulfillment. They have not found God's cause, but they are trying to feel like they at least are doing something of significance.

There is the problem of fewer whales in the seas, so

"Save the Whales" campaigns are really popular. Some people do not like the fact that dolphins are at Sea World, so they make a cause around setting them free. They cry, "Stop the dolphin slave trade!"

Others are really dismayed about cruelty to animals. As a result, there are many animal protection groups. One is called the Association for the Humane Treatment of Animals. They boast of having 1,750,000 members.[19] Think about it. They have 1,750,000 people involved in their cause of helping animals. Now, I am all for helping animals, but I want to help hurting people more. Could it be that they care more about helping animals than we care about helping hurting people? If they can get 1,750,000 people to save animals, can we not do more to save people?

There are so many other causes, from "Save the Spotted Owls" to "Save the Planet." All these groups raise millions of dollars to rally people to their cause. Isn't it amazing that we think nothing of getting something in the mail from a "Save the Whales" group asking for money to help them. But if we get a letter from a preacher wanting money to help save people, we get offended.

I heard a leader from Serbia speaking on the radio during the height of the Serbian war. He said, "If 100,000 penguins had washed up on the shore of a beach somewhere dead, every country in the world would be there to help figure out why. We have had more than 100,000 people die here, and no one seems to care." We need to begin to care about people like God does.

There are **life–threatening causes**. The wars in Vietnam, Nicaragua, and Yugoslavia were all a matter of rallying around a cause. Millions of people believed in a person or style of government so much that they were willing die for it! They put guns in their hands and said, "I am ready to kill or be killed for what I believe." If they can do that for a style of government, can we not do more for the cause of Christ?

Newsmen constantly put their lives at risk for the sake of a story. I have a friend who works for CNN. He was on one of the first jeeps that drove into Kuwait after the war. They could have driven over land mines on the way in. He risked his life for the sake of a piece of video.

I found a newspaper article about two men who were stoned to death in Somalia. They were out taking pictures one day for their newspaper. They got into the wrong neighborhood and people began throwing rocks at them. They were hailed as heroes by their paper. Think about it. They gave their lives for the sake of a newspaper article. If they can do that for a newspaper that is read one day and burned the next, can we not do more for the Word of God which will last forever?

There are **religious causes**. Muslims believe so strongly in Allah that they pray five times a day at specific times no matter where they are. I saw a man in the Dallas–Fort Worth airport bow down on his knees towards Mecca and pray right in front of everyone — right in the middle of the airport!

All Buddhist young men are encouraged to be monks for three months of their lives. They shave their heads and walk around in orange robes begging for food for three months. They make themselves out to be complete fools, and they do something crazy for a man named Buddha who died over 1,000 years ago and is still dead. If they can do that for someone who is still dead, can we not do more for someone who died and rose from the dead? If they can do that for three months can we not go one or two months to another country to share Jesus with others? (You don't even have to shave your head!!)

Hindus believe that as they do things to bring pain to themselves, their gods will be pleased with them. They will walk for a week in 110 degree weather, barefoot on the pavement, to try to please their gods. They will shove a spike through their tongue or cheeks to try to get the approval of their gods. If they can do these things for the sake of gods that do not even exist (for the sake of a lie), can we not do more for the sake of the one true God?

We are not trying to earn something from God (unlike

Somali mob retaliates against UN air attack on warlord

Newsmen stoned to death

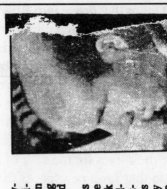

Killed . . . German photographer Hansl Kraus

MOGADISHU — An air attack by United Nations forces yesterday killed 16 Mogadishu residents and provoked a backlash in which at least two Western newsmen died.

American Cobra helicopter gunships blitzed what the UN said was a command centre of fugitive warlord Mohamed Farah Aideed and a rallying point for militia who have killed 35 UN "blue berets" in a month.

They said the raid had

been "flawless" and acknowledged that elders of Aideed's Haber Gedir clan were meeting in the building at the time although Aideed was not there.

A spokesman for Aideed's Somali National Alliance (SNA) claimed the attack killed 74 Somalis and wounded more than 200 but reporters saw only 16 bodies brought to their hotel by grieving Somalis in pickup trucks.

Angry mobs, incensed at the daylight attack on a city

photographer...
...ton.

centre house, turned upon reporters who had been taken to the bombed house by SNA sympathisers to record the horror.

Two photographers, Dan Eldon, a British-American national working for Reuters, and Hansi Krauss, a 30-year-old German working for Associated Press, were stoned to death.

Kenyans Hos Maina and Anthony Macharia, a photographer for Reuters and soundman for Reuters Television respectively, were missing when night fell and were presumed dead.

Angry mobs prevented their colleagues from visiting Mogadishu hospitals where they might have been taken and there was no way of verifying reports that their bodies had been dumped on the edge of the Bakarra market area.

There was no apparent reason why the crowd should have turned on reporters they have consistently used to publicise what they say is a vendetta against their clan and their leader, who vanished on June 17 and whose arrest is sought.

Angus Shaw, a reporter for Associated Press, said the crowd was passive when photographers who have recorded similar UN attacks for several weeks arrived at the burning compound.

"But there was a shot, or some shots, and the crowd turned violent. They started pummelling my car. I saw Eldon and Krauss swamped

● To Page 3 ☞

Newsmen stoned to death

● From Page 1

by people, a hundred or more, as my driver put his foot down and got away."

Mohamed Shaffi, a Kenyan Pakistani cameraman for Reuters Television, was shot twice by a gunman as he too fled the burning compound but managed to throw himself in a stranger's car and was driven to safety.

Eldon's body was identified at a US military hospital. Shaffi was evacuated to his home base, Nairobi, after being escorted to the UN airport by Pakistani troops.

Somalis said Eldon and Krauss were stoned by the mob. Maina and Macharia were last seen near the same area.

The editor-in-chief of Reuters, Mark Wood, said: "These are all individuals who won respect and admiration from their colleagues for their work and for their commitment to getting the news. We know their families were very proud of them."

He said that if three Reuter journalists had been killed, as seemed probable, it would be the highest death toll in one incident for Reuters for at least 25 years. — Sapa-Reuter-AFP.

other religions). We just love Him so much that we respond by reaching out to others.

God's Cause

So what is the cause of Christ? Simple: It is people. That is what God cares about. He wants the whole world — not part of it, all of it!

Jesus put it clearly, "And this gospel of the kingdom will be preached in the whole world as a testimony to all nations, and then the end will come" (Matt. 24:14). Basically, He said the end is not coming until everyone gets a chance to hear. He is so committed to His cause that He will not allow the world to end until everyone has a chance to learn about eternal life. We can talk about Jesus coming back, pray for it, look at our watches and expect it — but it is not going to happen until everyone has a chance to hear the gospel.

Jesus said it this way, "My food . . . is to do the will of him who sent me and to finish his work" (John 4:34). He said, basically, "This is My heart and passion. It is My oxygen, My drink, My food! It is all I think about! I have got to finish the task!"

God is looking for people today to get so involved that they would do anything to reach the world! He wants young people like you to get so caught up in HIS CAUSE that they would do anything to help everyone to know.

When you plug your life into the greatest CAUSE that has ever existed, you find real purpose. You find what you were born to do. You become a part of the most strategic invasion ever to hit this earth: the invasion of God's love. Join the cause now. Go on a mission trip. Help reach out to people who never in their lives have had a chance to hear! Take a month or two to pour your all into something that really matters. You can go this summer with Teen Mania Missions. Call us today for an application for our Summer or Christmas mission trips.

You will feel an incredible sense of purpose knowing that your life really counted for eternity!

19

Dream Big!

What is your dream? What do you want more than anything else? What do you really want to do with your life?

I am afraid that too many young people are not asking themselves this question. So many have been discouraged and disillusioned because of the circumstances surrounding their lives. As you have read the different chapters in this book, you have seen that there is certainly a lot that could get you down. But you also have seen that God has an answer for each issue. So, now it is time to ask the question, "What am I going to do with my life for God?"

God is looking for a generation of dreamers! He wants people who will dare to think the impossible. He is looking for young people who are ready to live on the edge for Him and do something great to change the world. It is time to stand up and take your place in history. It is time to start while you are young to leave something by which this world will remember you.

God uses ordinary people to do incredible things. It all starts with a dream. Every invention that was ever discovered, every ministry that was ever started, began with a dream. If you could do anything for God what would it be?

Proverbs 29:18 says, "Where there is no vision, the people perish . . ." (KJV). You have got to have a vision — a dream — if you want to accomplish all that God has for you. It is time to think big, pray big, and DREAM BIG!

How to Find Your Dream

Some people have been told for so long that they *"can't"* that they begin to believe it. We talked about how to overcome that feeling of helplessness and worthlessness in Chapter 14. You have already shown that you are a dreamer by the mere fact that you have made it to this point of the book. You are above average. You are looking for God's best. Get ready for the excursion of a lifetime!

If you are to find your dream, the first thing you need to think about is this: How does God dream? God always thinks BIG. A friend of mine says, "My God is too big to think dink." God thought of everything from the smallest chromosomes and DNA to the black holes in space when He dreamed about the universe. Psalm 92:5 says, ". . . how profound your thoughts!" When God thinks, He thinks in a big, wild, and adventurous way.

The Bible says you were created in His image. He has given you the ability to think like He does (1 Cor. 2:16). You have a God–given ability to imagine. In fact, Genesis 2:15 says that God put Adam in the Garden of Eden to work it and take care of it. This was Adam's job. He was to make it beautiful. He could do whatever He wanted to with it except eat of the one tree. Adam used his own imagination and named the animals. God wanted him to be creative and make the garden awesome.

Proverbs 15:26 tells us that the thoughts of the pure are pleasing to God. This means that if you are saved and walking with all your heart as closely as you possibly can to Jesus, He really is pleased with what you think. Proverbs 12:5 says, "The thoughts of the righteous are right . . ." (KJV). Let God use your thoughts — your ability to dream — to bring himself glory.

First you should begin to dream about your **personal life with Jesus**. What are your goals in your relationship with the Lord? What do you really want to be like? How much do you want to grow in Him this next year? What areas of your life do you want transformed? In what ways do you want your prayer and Bible–reading times to get better? Dream big about your walk with the Lord.

Next you should begin to dream about **the ministry that God has for you now**. What does God want to do through you this next year? How does He want to use you to change your school or work place? What could those hangouts in your town look like in a year if you started doing something right now? What about a mission trip? Think about all the people around the world who have never had a chance to hear about Jesus — then dream big about how you can get there to reach them.

Finally, you should begin to dream about **the future that God has for you**. What could you really do to have a lifelong impact for the kingdom of God? How many souls could be saved? How many churches started? How much money could you pump into missions with your life of service to God? Dream big about the incredible impact that your life can make.

It is not arrogant to dream big. God dreams big dreams. When you dream big, you are just like God. The more creative you are, the more you imitate your Heavenly Father. However, you might not want to tell everyone right up front like Joseph did (Gen. 37). If you tell everyone, you *could* sound like you are puffed up. God might give you a dream, but it's not ready for everyone else to hear until you get closer to the time of actually fulfilling your dream.

Remember that He is "… able to do immeasurably more than all we ask or imagine …" (Eph. 3:20). That means that if you can think it, God can do it. Another pointer is to never let money or location determine your dream. You might get a great idea, and then think, "But how could I ever get the money to do that?" Don't you dare let money stop you! I always tell teens who want to go on a mission trip, "God has all kinds of money, you just have to find out in whose pockets He's keeping it!" You may want to take some time right now while your ideas are fresh and write out your dreams for each of these different areas.

How to Go for It

Now that you have taken some time to write down some of the dreams that God has given you, it is time to do something about them. You must rearrange your schedule in order to accommodate your dreams. You have to set your priorities so that you accomplish what you set out to do. You have to plan into your life the opportunity to execute your ideas or they will never happen.

For example, if you want to have great quiet times, you have to plan what you will do during your time with God and how much time it will take. Set time aside and plan the things necessary to put together the ministry ideas that God has given you. If you do not force yourself to do it, you will live a life of regrets.

It is important to share your dreams with the right people. Do not cast your pearls before pigs, but you should share them with some trusted friends. You have to know that there are other people who believe in you, who are praying for you and standing with you. As I said earlier, don't be like Joseph and blab it all over town, but find some trusted confidants and let them in on what God is telling you to do. People may laugh at your dream, but if you know God spoke it to you, then keep your head up high and keep aiming for it. A number of people laughed at me when I wanted to go across the country to go to college, and then others laughed when we started Teen Mania. Still others mocked when we set really high goals for reaching the world. Today those people are not laughing anymore.

You have now come to the stage where you should write out the strategy of *how* you are going to make your dreams happen. You have already written out the dreams, now you have to think through all the ramifications. What should you do first? What comes next? Who else should you ask to get involved? How much will it cost? Where will you get the money? What should you do this week? This month? Each month this year? The next few years?

If God has given you a dream, then you have the

responsibility to plan a way to get it done. Don't worry, God will guide you as you plan (James 1:5).

You might say, "I think this is God's idea, but what if it is not? I will end up doing all these things in my own strength and it will all have been a waste." Very few people hear God in an audible voice. You have to trust in your ability to hear Him. If you are going to err, it would be better to err while you are doing something and getting people saved than by doing nothing. It is easier for God to steer a moving car than a parked one.

Decide to Go for It

Now that you have your dream and your plan written out, it is time to commit. If you haphazardly try to attempt to reach your goal, you never will. Hebrews 12:2 says that Jesus ". . . for the joy set before him endured the cross, scorning its shame, and sat down at the right hand of the throne of God."

Jesus knew what the ramifications would be and was ready to do whatever it would take to accomplish His goal. He knew it would not be easy — most worthwhile things are not easy. Are you ready to endure for your dream? You need to be resolute as Jesus was when He set out for Jerusalem (Luke 9:51). You just need to go for it.

When God gives you a dream, it is worth giving your all for it. It is time to go broke, lay everything on the table, and commit to do everything in your power to accomplish your dream. Commit to Him that as long as He continues to provide and His blessing is on you, you will complete the task He has given you.

God will keep His part of the deal (He always does) and you keep your part of the deal. When it is all said and done, this world will be a different place and you will have had a lot of fun doing it!

Commit today to pursue your dream.

20

God's Dream

God has a dream for our lives. First He wants us to be radically saved and set on fire for Him! He wants us to be thoroughly committed to loving Him and going after Him with all of our hearts. He wants to heal the brokenness in our lives and put us back together again. He wants us to live clean lives and have an undeniable passion for Him. The Bible says He wants to bless our lives and to give us abundant life (John 10:10)! This is where we usually stop, but this is where He just begins.

God wants to use your life to change this world in a big way! He is thinking about you and how He desires for you to be completely strong in Him, but He is also thinking about the rest of the world. God's dream has to do with reaching the "ends of the earth" (Acts 1:8). He has been wanting the whole world to know Him from the beginning. He never wanted just a part of the world, He wanted it all! He never wanted a few people, He wanted them all. He never wanted just the people in America to know Him, He wanted the whole world.

For thousands of years, God has been strategizing how He can get the world back. He is constantly thinking about it. We, as humans, think about many things. He thinks about one thing: the people of the world and how to reach them. He is specifically trying to reach those who have never had their first chance to hear about Him. His dream is that everyone would have a chance to hear.

Many, many people are caught up in the American dream. They love God but they also love the "stuff" that the affluence of North America offers. They spend so much time planning how to get what is supposed to bring happiness that they forget to *be* happy. Their life is going full steam ahead trying to achieve the American dream. They concentrate so much on fulfilling that dream that they don't even consider God's dream.

Jonah's Mistake

Jonah, as we know, was running from God's call on his life. God had called him to go to Ninevah, the capital of Assyria. He was supposed to be a missionary to the Ninevites. He was called to be a part of the most important thing in the heart of God. He was to go tell people who had never had a chance to hear about the truth.

When he decided to run from God's call, he was not simply running from a nice idea God had for him. He was trying to escape from doing **the most important assignment** in the history of mankind! He was trying to stand in the way of God's dream being fulfilled!

The Lord had even told him what to preach. He was supposed to tell them to repent or, basically, God would blow them off the face of the earth — just like Sodom and Gomorrah, Part Two. He did not even have to think of his own sermon!

God always has His way of getting His job done. We know that Jonah finally showed up in Ninevah after enduring the storm and hanging out in the belly of the fish for three days. The Bible says that he preached to the people in Ninevah, and everyone repented (Jon. 3:3–5). They all fasted and put on sackcloth and ashes. It says that even the animals fasted! Wow, that is serious!

Jonah was mad. He wanted to be remembered as the prophet who preached to a city that didn't repent with the result of the whole city being blown up. He cared more about how he looked in front of the people than he cared about the people themselves. After God had forgiven them, Jonah went outside the city onto a hill to look down on the people and complain.

There he was, out in the hot desert–like sun, just as mad as he could be. God decided to have some mercy on him. He grew up a plant while Jonah was sleeping so he could have some shade. Jonah woke up the next morning still angry, and he complained all day. God said, "Forget this," and the next day when Jonah woke up the plant was dead. Now Jonah was *really* mad!

God asked him in Jonah 4:9, " '. . . Do you have a right to be angry about the vine?' 'I do,' he said. 'I am angry enough to die.' " Jonah was so wrapped up in his plant, and whether he had shade, that he never caught God's heart for the people. He cared more about his reputation as a prophet than the people. He cared more about his own comfort than he did about the people.

God was trying to get Jonah to care about His dream, and all he cared about was himself. It is as if God was saying, "Jonah, can't you see? I have been trying to get you to care about all these people in Ninevah. Even after preaching to them you still missed the whole point! Shouldn't I care about them, Jonah? Of course, I should and so should **YOU!**"

It is time for us to start caring about God's dream for the world and not just about our own lives!

I am afraid that too many Christians are still like Jonah. We care more about our VCRs and our walkmans than about reaching others. We care more about whether God has answered our prayer for a new car than if He answered our prayer for reaching a country. We get mad when we do not have the answer and get what we want right away. "But, God, I prayed for that thing! Why isn't it here yet?" are the words God hears repeatedly. We are more concerned with whether we are comfortable than we are with God's passion to reach those who have never heard His gospel.

God wants us to care about what He cares about more than our own comfort. So what if we give up eating at McDonald's for a month while we go to the mission field!

(Besides, most countries have McDonald's anyway.) So maybe you have to sleep on a harder bed for a month or two. Is it worth it to reach people? Of course, it is.

God is looking for young people who will make His dream their utmost priority! They will do everything it takes to make it happen. They are consumed with a passion to do everything they can to make His dream a reality while they are on this earth! Will you dare to live God's dream?

It really is only His dream which matters. Nothing else is even a close second. The only thing that matters is accomplishing all that God wants.

Paul's Ambition

Paul said in Romans 15:20, "It has always been my ambition to preach the gospel where Christ was not known. ..." Basically, he says, "I want to go where no one else wants to go. It's my passion, my heart, my soul, my everything, to go and preach where no one ever has before."

Paul just could not be happy doing what all the other Christians were doing. He could not just hang around church picnics and youth group outings. He had to do *something* that would change the world! Something was burning in his heart to let others know about the thing that had so drastically changed his life. He could not just blend in and pretend that nothing had happened.

What are your ambitions? What are you aspiring to achieve with your life? God is looking for a generation of young people who really care about what He cares about. He wants us to make His dream our dream! Then we will begin to pour all our guts into accomplishing the only thing that really matters anyway.

The result of His dream is described in Revelation 7:9, "After this I looked and there before me was a great multitude that no-one could count, from every nation, tribe, people and language, standing before the throne and in front of the Lamb...." This is God's dream come true. He gets His way after all!

It does not matter what it costs; it is only God's dream

that matters. It does not matter what we have to give up, where we have to move, where we have to go, how illogical it may seem, or how much everyone else may not understand. It is only God's dream that is worth pouring your life into.

Some people might think, "Come on, I just want to have a little fun! This is too serious for a teenage Christian." Jesus did not die so that we could have good clean fun! He wants everyone to know Him, and it is time that we as His family start aiming at getting them all into the kingdom of God! This is a serious calling we have. Besides, I cannot think of any more fun than Paul and Silas had talking about what was going to happen for the Lord in their next village! Now that is HOLY FUN!

About 43 percent of the world's population is currently under 20 years of age.[20] It takes young people to reach young people. Are you ready? It is your turn to make your mark on the world for Jesus! Would you dare to go and get involved personally in making God's dream come true?

For God so loved the world that He . . . No, He DID NOT send a fax to let us know. He sent His son! He sent a person. Today, God still sends people. He does not just want some of our money to go; He wants US to go! He does not just want tracts and Bibles to go overseas; He wants flesh and blood to go.

When you personally reach out and put your arms around those who have never heard, you will touch a little bit of His dream. When you personally look into the eyes of a man or woman who has never had a chance to hear the gospel, and you watch them go from darkness to light, you make a discovery: You discover what it feels like to be involved in the most important adventure since the beginning of mankind. You are helping God's dream become a reality and there is nothing like it!

Make plans now to do something about changing the world. Write or call Teen Mania Ministries to get an application to go on a mission trip. We take teens of all

ages as well as young adults to countries around the world during summer and Christmas breaks. Right now is the time to start living God's dream!

Notes

[1] *The New Research,* Rockford Institute, Nov. 1990, page 2-4.

[2] *Fundamentalist Journal,* Oct. 1984.

[3] Neil T. Anderson and Steve Russo, *Seduction of Our Children* (Eugene, OR: Harvest House Publishers, Inc., 1991), page 90.

[4] *Facets,* July 1989, page 1.

[5] *The New Research,* Nov. 1990, page 2-4.

[6] *Dallas Morning News,* Oct. 11, 1987.

[7] Patrick Johnstone, *Operation World* (Grand Rapids, MI: Zondervan Publishing House, 1993).

[8] "STD Hotline," *Medical Aspects of Human Sexuality,* Feb. 1991, page 60.

[9] "Sharp Rise in Rare Sex-Related Diseases," *New York Times Health,* July 14, 1988, page 234.

[10] Jonathan Zenilman, M.D., "Sexually Transmitted Disease in Homosexual Adolescents," *Journal of Adolescent Health Care,* 1988, vol. 9, no. 2, page 129-130.

[11] Barbara Kantrowitz, "The Dangers of Doing It," *Newsweek,* special issue, summer/fall 1990, page 56-57.

[12] Kim Painter, "Syphilis Cases Hit 41-Year Peak," *USA Today,* Feb. 2, 1990, page 1D.

[13] "Sleeping with the Enemy," *Newsweek,* Dec. 8, 1991, page 58-59.

[14] Prodigy Services Company, April 1992.

[15] *Pastor's Weekly Briefing,* Sept. 2, 1994, vol. 2, no. 35.

[16] "Teens at High Risk for Mental Illness," *USA Today,* Oct. 9, 1990, page 1D.

[17] *MTV Examined,* Reel to Real Ministries.

[18] *Focus on the Family,* August 1994, page 2-4.

[19] *Encyclopedia of Associations 1995,* (Detroit, MI: Gale Research, Inc., 1994), 29th edition, vol. 1, part 2, page 1363.

[20] United Nations Population Trends Division, 1990 figures.

Notes

By the grace of God and for His glory, I commit my entire life to obeying His commission of Matthew 28:18-20 wherever and however He leads me, giving priority to the people currently beyond the reach of the gospel (Rom. 15:20-21).
I will also endeavor to impart this vision to others.

_____

signed

_____

date

Teen Mania Ministries conducts conventions across North America called Acquire the Fire. If your teen or youth group would like information about how to attend one in your area, please give us a call.

We also take teenagers on summer mission trips for either a four or eight-week period (we have a two-week trip for groups of 15 or more to Mexico). We provide all the leadership, meals, travel arrangements, lodging, and ministry tools (for example, drama and tracts) so that your teens can be effective in ministry.

Write us today for information on either our summer or Christmas-break trips. We have taken thousands of teens over the years, and have documented more than 300,000 people who have given their lives to Jesus through these teens.

It is time for your kids to get in on the action!

Contact us at:

Teen Mania Ministries
P.O. Box 700721
Tulsa, OK 74170-0721
(918) 496-1891
1-800-299-TEEN

TEEN MANIA INTERNSHIP

Get real. What is real?
It's not what you think. The internship isn't for wimps.
Don't think it'll be a cushioned year. It won't be.
Don't think it's a free ride. It's not.
Think tough. Think intense. Think long, hard hours.
Think God. Think relationships.
Think change — there's no room for mediocrity.
It's a challenge.
It's a move from comfort to the edge.
Kinda like skydiving.
It's a consecration to God, a choice to go beyond what
you ever thought possible. It's your chance to say yes.
It builds character. Induces change. Won't allow you to
stay the same. Builds faith.
Are you ready to move? Are you ready to change?
Are you ready to go beyond?
Are you ready to get real?

Hebrews 10:39
". . . for we are not of those who shrink
back and are destroyed, but of those
who believe and are saved."

Detach and mail to Teen Mania Ministries, P.O. Box 700721, Tulsa, OK 74170-0721

Internship Mini-Application
to begin: ❏ August   ❏ January

Name_____Age _____

Address _____

City_____State_____Zip _____

Home Phone_(____)_____Years of school completed_____

Church Name_____Phone (____)_____

Have you ever been on a Teen Mania Trip before? _____